Guitar Chord Songbook

Crosby, Stills & Nash

Cover photo provided by Photofest

ISBN 978-1-4234-9204-7

HAL•LEONARD®
CORPORATION
7777 W. BLUEMOUND RD. P.O. BOX 13819 MILWAUKEE, WI 53213

Visit Hal Leonard Online at
www.halleonard.com

Guitar Chord Songbook

Contents

Almost Cut My Hair

Words and Music by
David Crosby

Melody:

Al-most   cut my hair. __

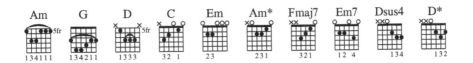

Am   G   D   C   Em   Am*   Fmaj7   Em7   Dsus4   D*

Intro

‖: **Am**   **G** |**D**   :‖

Verse 1

Am   **G**   **D**
Almost   cut my hair.

Am G   **D**
      It happened just the other day.

Am G   **D**
      It's gettin' kind ___ a long.

Am   **G**   **D**
   I could've   said it was in my way.

         C   **Em**   **Am***
But I didn't and   I wonder why.

        Fmaj7   **Em7**
I feel like   letting my freak flag ___ fly.

      Dsus4   **D***
Yes, I   feel like I owe it, to someone.

Guitar Solo 1   ‖: Am   G | D   :‖ *Play 4 times*

Verse 2

Am   G   D
     Must be because I had   the flu for Christ - mas.

Am   G   D
     And I'm not   feeling up to par.

Am   G   D
     It increases my paranoia.

Am   G   D
     Like looking into my mirror and seein' a police car.

            C   Em   Am*
But I'm not   giving in ____ an inch to fear.

      Fmaj7   Em7
'Cause I   promised myself this year.

    Dsus4   D*
I ____ feel like I owe it to someone.

Guitar Solo 2   ‖: Am   G | D   :‖ *Play 6 times*

Verse 3

Am G D
             When I fin'lly get myself together

Am G   D
        I'm gonna get down in that sunny, southern weather.

          C   Em   Am*
And I'll find   a place inside ____ and laugh.

Fmaj7   Em7
     Separate the wheat ____ from the chaff.

Dsus4 D*   Am G D
     I feel   like I owe it ____   to someone, yeah.

Outro   ‖: Am   G | D   :‖ *Repeat and fade*

Anything at All

Words and Music by
David Crosby

Melody:

An - y-thing you wan - na know, —

(Capo 1st fret)

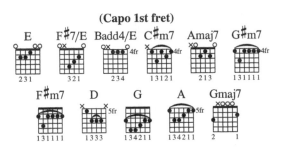

E   F#7/E   Badd4/E   C#m7   Amaj7   G#m7

F#m7   D   G   A   Gmaj7

Intro

| E   F#7/E | Badd4/E   F#7/E |

Verse 1

E   F#7/E   Badd4/E   F#7/E
Anything you wanna know,   just ask me.

      E   F#7/E   Badd4/E   F#7/E
I'm the world's ____ most opinion - ated man.

            C#m7
I'll give you an answer if I can.

            Amaj7   G#m7 F#m7
Catch one passing   through that feels right for you.

Verse 2

E   F#7/E   Badd4/E   F#7/E
Anything you wanna know,   just ask me,

      C#m7
It's worth ev'ry cent it costs.

      Amaj7   G#m7   F#m7
And you know it's free for you. ____ Special deal.

Bridge

C#m7 D G A
Ah, ah, ___ oh, oh.

C#m7 D G Gmaj7 A
Feel _____ feelin' good.

C#m7 D G
Ah. Le, le, le, la, la, la, la.

Verse 3

E F#7/E Badd4/E F#7/E
Anything you wanna know, it should be perfectly clear.

C#m7
You see just beneath the surface of the mud.

Amaj7 G#m7 F#m7
There's more mud here, surprise.

Verse 4

E F#7/E Badd4/E F#7/E
Is there anything you wanna know, on any subject at all?

C#m7 Amaj7 G#m7 F#m7
I've got time for one more question here be - fore I fall, fall.

N.C. C#m7
Is there anything at all?

Carry Me

Words and Music by
David Crosby

Drop D tuning:
(low to high) D-A-D-G-B-E

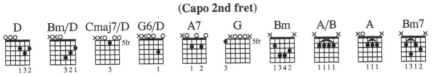

Melody:

When I was a young _ man _

(Capo 2nd fret)

D   Bm/D   Cmaj7/D   G6/D   A7   G   Bm   A/B   A   Bm7

Intro   ‖: D |Bm/D |Cmaj7/D   G6/D |D   :‖

Verse 1

   D   **A7**
   When I was a young man

   G   **Bm   A/B**
   I found an old dream.

   D   **A**
   Was as battered and worn a one

   G   **Bm   A   G**
   As you have ever seen.

   D   **A**
   Now I made it some __ new wings,

   G   **Bm7   A   G**
   And I painted the nose.

   D   **A**
   And I wished so hard,

           G   Bm   A   G
   Up in the air ___ I ro - se singing,

Chorus 1

D   Bm/D
   "Carry me, carry me, yeah.

Cmaj7/D G6/D   D
Carry me   above the world.

           Bm/D
Carry me, oo, carry me.

Cmaj7/D G6/D D
Carry me."

Verse 2

D   A
   And I once loved a ___ girl,

G   Bm A/B
   And she was younger than me.

D   A
   Her parents kept her locked   up in their life,

           G
And she was crying at night.

                  Bm   A   G
She was wishing she could ___ be ___ free.

D   A
   'Course I most - ly remember her laughing,

G   Bm A G
   Standing there watching us play.

D   A   G
   For a while there ___ the mu - sic

   Bm A   G
Would take her away ___ and she'd be singing,

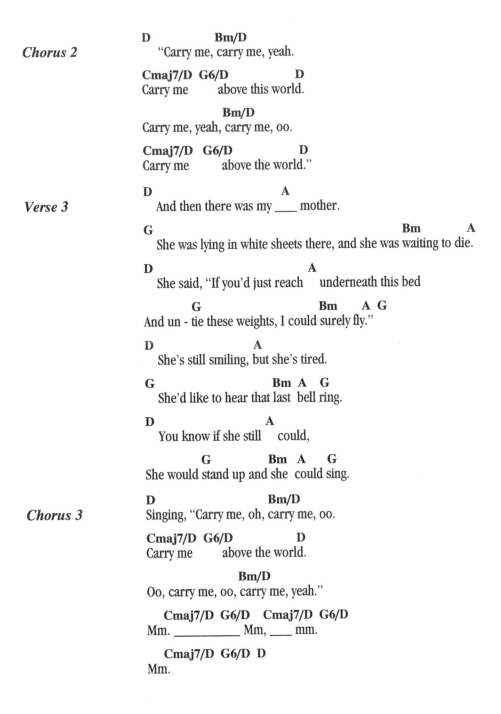

Chorus 2

   D   Bm/D
    "Carry me, carry me, yeah.

Cmaj7/D G6/D   **D**
Carry me   above this world.

              Bm/D
Carry me, yeah, carry me, oo.

Cmaj7/D G6/D   **D**
Carry me   above the world."

Verse 3

D   A
    And then there was my ____ mother.

G   Bm   A
    She was lying in white sheets there, and she was waiting to die.

D   A
    She said, "If you'd just reach   underneath this bed

           G   Bm   A G
And un - tie these weights, I could surely fly."

D   A
    She's still smiling, but she's tired.

G   Bm A G
    She'd like to hear that last bell ring.

D   A
    You know if she still   could,

           G   Bm A   G
She would stand up and she could sing.

Chorus 3

D   Bm/D
Singing, "Carry me, oh, carry me, oo.

Cmaj7/D G6/D   **D**
Carry me   above the world.

          Bm/D
Oo, carry me, oo, carry me, yeah."

  Cmaj7/D G6/D   Cmaj7/D G6/D
Mm. _____ Mm, ____ mm.

  Cmaj7/D G6/D D
Mm.

Carry On

Words and Music by
Stephen Stills

One morn - ing   I   woke _ up

Open E5 tuning, down 1/2 step:
(low to high) E♭-E♭-E♭-E♭-B♭-E♭

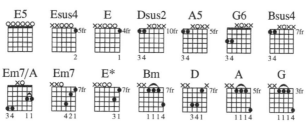

Intro   ‖: E5 Esus4 E Esus4 E E5 │Esus4 E Esus4 E E5 :‖ *Play 4 times*

Verse 1

Dsus2   A5   G6
  One morning   I woke up   and I knew

        E5   Esus4 E Esus4 E E5 Esus4 E Esus4 E E5
You were really gone.

Dsus2   A5   G6   E5
  A new day,   a new way,   and new eyes

   Esus4 E Esus4 E E5 Esus4 E Esus4 E E5
To see   the dawn.

Bsus4   Dsus2   A5   Em7/A
Go your way, ___ I'll go ___ mine   and carry on.

Interlude 1   ‖: E5 Esus4 E Esus4 E E5 │Esus4 E Esus4 E E5 :‖

Verse 2

Dsus2   A5   G6
  The sky   is clearing   and the night

       E5   Esus4 E Esus4 E E5 Esus4 E Esus4 E E5
Has cried ___ e - nough.

Dsus2   A5   G6
  The sun,   he come,   the world

     E5   Esus4 E Esus4 E E5 Esus4 E Esus4 E E5
To sof - ten up.

   Bsus4   Dsus2   A5   Em7/A
Rejoice, ___ rejoice, ___ we have ___ no choice but ___ to carry on.

Interlude 2	*Repeat Interlude 1*

Verse 3

   Dsus2   **A5**   **G6**
   The fortunes   of fables   are able

    E5   **Esus4 E Esus4 E E5 Esus4 E Esus4 E E5**
To sing the song.

  Dsus2   **A5**   **G6**
  Now witness the   quickness   with which

    E5   **Esus4 E Esus4 E E5 Esus4 E Esus4 E E5**
We get a - long.

        Bsus4   **Dsus2**   **A5**   **Em7/A**
To sing ____ the blues __ you've got __ to live the dues

And carry on.

Interlude 3	*Repeat Intro*

Bridge

E5
Carry on, love is coming.

N.C.
Love is coming to us all.

Organ Solo   ‖: **N.C.(Em7)** | | | :‖

Guitar Solo 1 ‖: **N.C.(Em7)** | | | :‖

Verse 4

E*   **Bm**
Where are you going now, ___ my love?

D   **N.C.(Em7)**
  Where will you be tomor - row?

E*   **Bm**
Will you bring me hap - piness?

D   **N.C.(Em7)**
Will you bring me sorrow?

Chorus 1

<pre>
        E*   D Bm   A
Oh, the questions of a thousand dreams,

E*   D   Bm   A
What you do and what you see.

E*   D   A G
Lover, can you talk   to me?
</pre>

Guitar Solo 2   *Repeat Guitar Solo 1*

Verse 5

<pre>
E*   Bm
Girl, when I was on my own

D   N.C.(Em7)
   Chasing you down,

E*   Bm
   What was it made you run?

D   N.C.(Em7)
Trying your best just to get around
</pre>

Chorus 2

<pre>
          E*   D Bm   A
The ques - tions of a thousand dreams,

E*   D   Bm   A
What you do and what you see.

E*   D   A G
Lover, can you talk   to me?
</pre>

Outro-Guitar Solo   *Repeat Guitar Solo 1 and fade*

Cathedral

Words and Music by
Graham Nash

Melody:

Six o'-clock   in the morn-ing, I   feel pret-ty good

(Capo 4th fret)

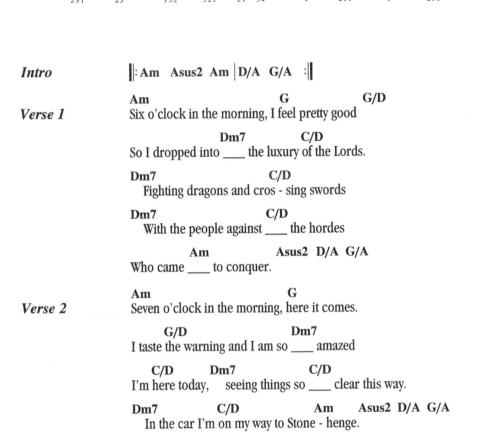

Am   Asus2   D/A   G/A   G   G/D   Dm7   C/D   Dm

Intro

‖: Am Asus2 Am | D/A G/A :‖

Verse 1

Am   G   G/D
Six o'clock in the morning, I feel pretty good

             Dm7   C/D
So I dropped into ___ the luxury of the Lords.

Dm7   C/D
  Fighting dragons and cros - sing swords

Dm7   C/D
  With the people against ___ the hordes

           Am   Asus2 D/A G/A
Who came ___ to conquer.

Verse 2

Am   G
Seven o'clock in the morning, here it comes.

     G/D   Dm7
I taste the warning and I am so ___ amazed

    C/D   Dm7   C/D
I'm here today,   seeing things so ___ clear this way.

Dm7   C/D   Am   Asus2 D/A G/A
  In the car I'm on my way to Stone - henge.

| Am Asus2 Am | D/A G/A |

Verse 3

Am   G   G/D
I'm flying in Win - chester Cathe - dral.

Am   G   G/D
Sunlight pouring through the break ___ of day.

Am   G   G/D
Stumbled through the door and in - to the cham - ber.

       Dm7   C/D
There's a lady setting flowers on the ta - ble. *Covered lace.*

       Dm7   C/D
And a clean - er in the distance finds a cob - web on a face.

       Dm7
And a feel - ing deep inside of me

       C/D   Am   Asus2   Am   D/A   G/A
Tells me this can't be the place.

Verse 4

Am   G   G/D
Come flying in Win - chester Cathe - dral.

Am   G   G/D
All religion has to have ___ its day.

Am   G   G/D
Expressions on the face ___ of the Sav - ior

       Dm7   C/D   Dm7   C/D
Made me say,   "I can't stay."

Chorus 1

Am   G
Open up the gates of the church and let me out ___ of here.

       Am
Too many people have lied in the name of Christ

    G
For anyone to heed the call.

       Am
So many people have died in the name of Christ

       G
That I can't believe it all.

       Dm
Now I'm standing on the grave of a soldier that died in 1799.

In the day he died it was a birthday and I noticed it was mine.

And my head didn't know just who I was and I went spinning back in time.

       Am   G
And I am high upon the altar,

       Am   G   Dm7   G/D   Dm7   C/D
High ___ upon the altar, high.

Verse 5

Am   G   G/D
I'm flying in Win - chester Cathe - dral.

Am   G   G/D
It's hard enough to drink ___ the wine.

Am   G   G/D
The air inside just hangs in illusion.

          Dm7 C/D   Dm7 C/D
But given time,   I'll be fine.

Chorus 2

Am   G
Open up the gates of the church and let me out ___ of here.

          Am
Too many people have lied in the name of Christ

  G
For anyone to heed the call.

          Am
Too many people have died in the name of Christ

    G
That I can't believe it all.

          Dm
Now I'm standing on the grave of a soldier that died in 1799.

In the day he died it was a birthday and I noticed it was mine.

And my head didn't know just who I was and I went spinning back in time.

          Am   G   Am   G   Dm7 G/D
And I am high upon the altar, high ___ upon the altar, high.

Outro   ‖: Dm7 |C/D :‖ *Play 3 times*
              | Am   ‖

Chicago

Words and Music by
Graham Nash

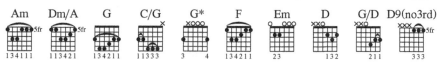

Am   Dm/A   G   C/G   G*   F   Em   D   G/D   D9(no3rd)

Intro   ‖: Am   Dm/A   Am   Dm/A :‖ *Play 4 times*

Verse 1
           Am   Dm/A   Am
So your brother's bound and gagged

Dm/A   Am   Dm/A   Am
And they've chained him to a chair.

Dm/A   G   C/G   G   C/G   Am   Dm/A   Am
Won't you please __ come to Chica - go just to sing?

Dm/A   Am   Dm/A   Am
In a   land   that's known as free - dom,

Dm/A   Am   Dm/A   Am
How can such a thing __ be   fair?

Dm/A   G   C/G   G
Won't you please __ come to Chica - go

C/G   Am   Dm/A   Am
For the help __ that we can bring?

Chorus 1
          G*   F   Em
We can change ___ the world,

          G*   F   Em
Rearrange _____ the world.

      D   G/D   D9(no 3rd)   G/D
It's dying

        Am   Dm/A   Am   Dm/A
To get better.

| Am   Dm/A   Am   Dm/A |

Verse 2

> Am Dm/A   Am   Dm/A
> Politi - cians, sit ___ yourselves down,
>
>   Am   Dm/A Am
> There's nothing for you here.
>
> Dm/A   G   C/G   G C/G Am Dm/A Am Dm/A
> Won't you please ___ come to Chica - go for a   ride?
>
> Am   Dm/A   Am
> Don't ask Jack to help ___ you
>
> Dm/A   Am   Dm/A Am
> 'Cause he'll turn the oth - er ear.
>
> Dm/A   G   C/G   G
> Won't you please ___ come to Chica - go
>
> C/G   Am   Dm/A Am
> Or else join the oth - er side?

Chorus 2

>   G*   F   Em
> (We can change) Yes, we can change the world,
>
>   G*   F   Em
> (Rearrange ___) Rear-range the world.
>
>   D   G/D
> (It's dying.) If you believe ___ in justice
>
>   D9(no3rd)   G/D
> (It's dying.) And if you believe ___ in freedom,
>
>   D   G/D
> (It's dying.) Let a man live his own life.
>
>   D9(no3rd)   G/D   G*
> (It's dying.)   Rules and reg - ulations, who needs them?
>
> F
> Open up the door.

Interlude   ‖: Am   Dm/A Am   Dm/A :‖ *Play 4 times*

                        Am   Dm/A   Am

Verse 3   Somehow peo - ple ___ must ___ be free.

                        Dm/A Am   Dm/A   Am
                        I   hope the day __ comes __ soon.

                        Dm/A   G   C/G   G
                        Won't you please __ come to Chica - go?

                        C/G   Am Dm/A Am
                        Show your face.

                        Dm/A Am   Dm/A   Am
                        From the bottom of __ the o - cean

                        Dm/A   Am   Dm/A   Am
                        To the moun - tains of __ the moon,

                        Dm/A   G   C/G   G
                        Won't you please __ come to Chica - go?

                        C/G Am   Dm/A   Am
                        No one else can take __ your place.

Chorus 3   *Repeat Chorus 2*

Change Partners

Words and Music by
Stephen Stills

All of the la - dies at-tend - ing the ball

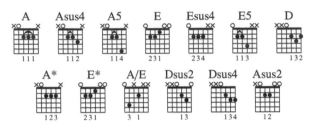

Intro

|A Asus4 |A5 Asus4 A Asus4|A Asus4 |

|A5 Asus4 A Asus4|E Esus4 |E5 |

Verse 1

    A   Asus4   A5   Asus4
All of the la - dies attend - ing the ball

        A   Asus4   A5
Are request - ed to gaze ___ in the faces

    Asus4   E   Esus4 E5 Esus4
Found on your dance cards.

   A   Asus4   A5   Asus4 A   Asus4
Please, then remem - ber and don't get too close to one special one.

    A5   Asus4   E Esus4 E5
He will take your defens - es and run.

Chorus 1

N.C.   D   A*   E*
  So we change ___ part - ners.

       D   A* E*
Time to change ___ partners.

      D   A* A/E   E   D Dsus2 Dsus4 D Dsus2
You must change ___ partners a - gain.

Interlude 1

|A Asus4 |A5 Asus4 A Asus4|A Asus4 |

|A5 Asus4 A Asus4|E Esus4 |E5 Esus4 E |

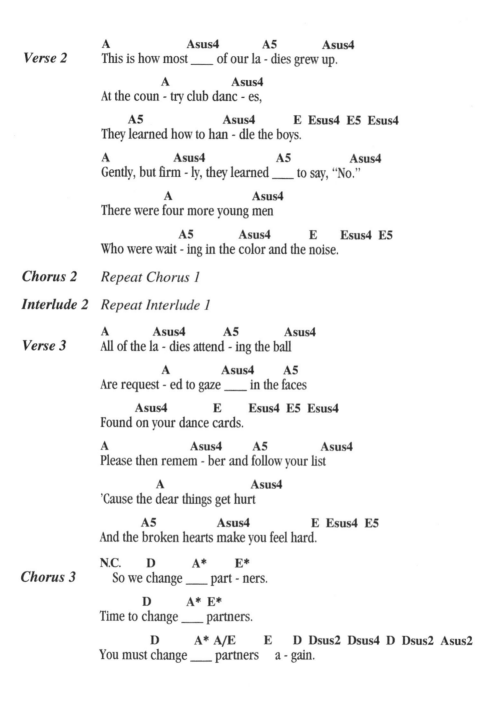

Verse 2

   A   Asus4   A5   Asus4
This is how most ___ of our la - dies grew up.

         A   Asus4
At the coun - try club danc - es,

      A5   Asus4   E Esus4 E5 Esus4
They learned how to han - dle the boys.

   A   Asus4   A5   Asus4
Gently, but firm - ly, they learned ___ to say, "No."

        A   Asus4
There were four more young men

         A5   Asus4   E   Esus4 E5
Who were wait - ing in the color and the noise.

Chorus 2   *Repeat Chorus 1*

Interlude 2   *Repeat Interlude 1*

Verse 3

   A   Asus4   A5   Asus4
All of the la - dies attend - ing the ball

      A   Asus4   A5
Are request - ed to gaze ___ in the faces

      Asus4   E   Esus4 E5 Esus4
Found on your dance cards.

   A   Asus4   A5   Asus4
Please then remem - ber and follow your list

       A   Asus4
'Cause the dear things get hurt

      A5   Asus4   E Esus4 E5
And the broken hearts make you feel hard.

Chorus 3

N.C.   D   A*   E*
 So we change ___ part - ners.

       D   A* E*
Time to change ___ partners.

      D   A* A/E   E   D Dsus2 Dsus4 D Dsus2 Asus2
You must change ___ partners a - gain.

Dark Star

Words and Music by
Stephen Stills

Melody:

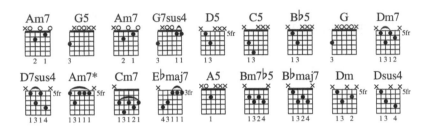

For - give me if ___ my fan - ta - sies _

| Am7 | G5 | Am7 | G7sus4 | D5 | C5 | Bb5 | G | Dm7 |
| D7sus4 | Am7* | Cm7 | Ebmaj7 | A5 | Bm7b5 | Bbmaj7 | Dm | Dsus4 |

Intro   ‖: N.C.(Am7) |(G5)   :‖ *Play 4 times*

Verse 1

     Am7   G7sus4
For - give me if my fantasies might seem a little shop worn.

      Am7   G7sus4
I'm sure you've heard it all before. I wonder what's the right form.

Am7   G7sus4
Love songs written for you, it's been going down for years.

     Am7   G7sus4
But to sing what's in my heart seems more honest than the tears.

      D5   C5   Bb5
I am curious,   don't want to hurry us.

C5   D5
    I'm intrigued ___ with us.

C5   Bb5
    Ain't this song ___ a bust?

C5 G   Dm7   D7sus4 Dm7
    I don't care, Dark Star.

Verse 2

Dm7   Am7*
I met you several years ___ ago.

    Cm7   Ebmaj7
The times, ___ they were so strange

       Dm7 D7sus4 Dm7
But I had that feel - ing.

         Am7*
You looked into my eyes ___ just once,

    Cm7   Ebmaj7   Dm7
An in - stant flashing by ___ that we were steal - ing.

        Am7*
Another time you felt ___ so bad

    Cm7   Ebmaj7   Dm7
And I wasn't any help ___ at all, as I recall.

         Am7*
We didn't know quite what ___ to do,

    Cm7   Ebmaj7   Dm7
So we left the wanting be ___ still there for me and you.

Chorus 1

A5   C5
Dark Star, I see you in the morning.

A5   C5
Dark Star, a, sleepin' next to me.

A5   C5
Dark Star, let the mem - 'ry of the evening

    Bm7b5   Bbmaj7
Be the first thing that you think of when you open up your smile

       Dm7   D7sus4 Dm7
And see me, Dark Star.

Verse 3

       Dm7   Am7*
It's easy to be with ___ you,

      Cm7   Ebmaj7
Even with the storms that rage

                   Dm7   D7sus4 Dm7
Beneath your search ___ for peace.

                      Am7*
We must make some time togeth - er,

         Cm7   Ebmaj7   Dm7
Take the kids ___ and find a world ___ that's ours ___ to keep.

                  Am7*
And now you got me dream - in', girl.

        Cm7   Ebmaj7   Dm7   D7sus4 Dm7
It's been so long, I thought ___ that I'd forgot - ten how.

              Am7*
My heart is once again ___ my soul.

       Cm7   Ebmaj7
We touched, we did, you know ___ we did.

           Dm7   D7sus4 Dm7
No more teas - ing now.

Chorus 2

A5   C5
Dark Star, I see you in the morning.

A5   C5
Dark Star, sleepin' next to me.

A5   C5
Dark Star, let the mem - 'ry of the evening

     Bm7b5   Bbmaj7
Be the first thing that you think of when you open up your smile

           Dm7   D7sus4 Dm7 D7sus4
And see me, Dark Star.

| *Piano Solo* | |Dm7 Am7* |Cm7 E♭maj7 |Dm7 | | D7sus4 | |
| | |Dm7 Am7* |Cm7 E♭maj7 |Dm7 | | | |

| *Guitar Solo* | ‖:Dm7 Am7* |Cm7 E♭maj7 |Dm7 | | :‖ |

Chorus 3

A5   C5
Dark Star, I see you in the morning.

A5   C5
Dark Star, a, sleepin' next to me.

A5   C5
Dark Star, let the mem'ry of the evening

   Bm7♭5   B♭maj7
Be the first thing that you think of when you open up your smile

        Dm7   D7sus4 Dm7
And see me, Dark Star.

       Cm7   Bm7♭5
Let the mem'ry of the evening be the first ___ thing that you think of

       B♭maj7
When you open up your smile

        Dm7   D7sus4 Dm Dsus4
And see me, Dark Star.

| *Outro* | |Dm Dsus4 |Dm Dsus4 |Dm Dsus4 |Dm | ‖ |

Daylight Again

Words and Music by
Stephen Stills

Melody:

Day - light _____ a - gain _____

Double Drop D tuning:
(low to high) D-A-D-G-B-D

Gm   D5   D5*   Dm9   C   G   F   Dm   Cadd9/E   Csus2

Intro

| Gm   D5 | D5* | Gm   D5 |
| 2/4 N.C.(Dm9) | 4/4 | D5* | |

Verse 1

Gm D5   D5*
Day - light a - gain

Gm   D5   D5*
Following me to bed.

 Gm   D5*   C
I think about ____ a hundred years ago

G   F   D5* Gm D5 N.C.(Dm9) D5*
 How ____ my father's bled.

Verse 2

 Gm   D5   D5*
I think I see a val - ley

Gm   D5   D5*
Covered with bones in blue.

Gm   D5   D5*   C
All the brave soldiers that cannot get older

      G   F   D5* Gm D5 Dm Cadd9/E Csus2 D5*
Been   as - kin' after you.

Verse 3

Gm   D5   D5*
Here ____ the past a cal - lin'

   Gm   D5   D5*
From Arm -   ageddon's side.

     Gm   D5   D5*   C
When ev'ryone's talkin' and no one is listenin'

G   F   D5* Gm D5 N.C.(Dm9) D5*
 How ____ can we de - cide?

N.C.
Do we find the cost of freedom buried in the ground?

Mother Earth will swallow you, lay your body down.

Déjà Vu

Words and Music by
David Crosby

If I had ev - er been here be - fore, I would

Open Em11 tuning:
(low to high) E-B-D-G-A-D

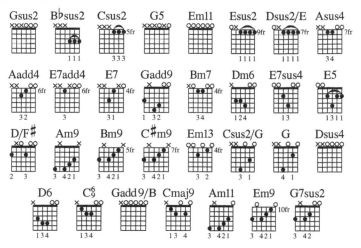

False Start

‖: Gsus2 B♭sus2 Gsus2 Csus2 :‖ *Play 11 times*
   w/ ad lib scat vocals

| Gsus2 B♭sus2 Gsus2 Csus2 | G5 |
   One,   two,   three,   four.

Intro

‖: Gsus2 B♭sus2 Gsus2 Csus2 :‖ *Play 4 times*

Verse 1

Gsus2 B♭sus2 Gsus2   Csus2
If I   had ever been here be - fore,

        Gsus2 B♭sus2   Gsus2 Csus2
I would probably know just what to do.

Gsus2 B♭sus2 Gsus2 Csus2 Gsus2 B♭sus2 Gsus2 Csus2
Don't you?

Gsus2 B♭sus2 Gsus2   Csus2
If I   had ever been here be - fore

        Gsus2   B♭sus2   Gsus2
On an - other time around the wheel,

 Csus2   Gsus2   B♭sus2 Gsus2 Csus2
I would prob'bly know just how to deal

Gsus2 B♭sus2 Gsus2 Csus2 Gsus2 B♭sus2 Gsus2 Csus2
With all of   you.

Bridge

Em11   Esus2 Dsus2/E
And I feel

Asus4 Aadd4 Asus4   Aadd4 Asus4 Aadd4
               Like I've been

E7add4   E7 E7add4 E7 E7add4 E7
Here be - fore.

        Esus2 Dsus2/E
Feel

Asus4 Aadd4 Asus4   Aadd4 Asus4 Aadd4
               Like I've been

E7add4   E7 E7add4 E7 E7add4 E7
Here be - fore.   And,   you

Gadd9   Bm7
Know, it makes me ___ wonder.

Dm6   E7sus4 E5 E7sus4 E5   D/F♯
   What's going on   un   -   der the ground?

           Em11   D/F♯
Mm, mm, mm. ___ (Do you know? Don't you wonder?)

Em11   Am9 Bm9 C♯m9
Mm, what's going on down under you?

	Em13 Csus2/G G Dsus4
Interlude	Da, da, da, ___ da, da, da, da, ___ da, da, da.

D6 C6/9 Gadd9/B C6/9 Dsus4
Da, da, da,   da.

Em11 C6/9 Cmaj9 Am11
Da.

Outro |Em9 |Bm9 |Am9 |G7sus2 |

    Em11
‖:   (We have all been here before. We have all been here before.)

|Em9 |Bm9 |Am9 |G7sus2 :‖

Em11   **Em9 Bm9**
(We have all been here before. We have all been here before.)

Delta

Words and Music by
David Crosby

Melody:

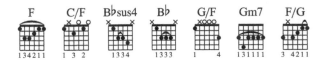

Wak-ing   stream of con - scious-ness

F	C/F	Bbsus4	Bb	G/F	Gm7	F/G
134211	1 3 2	1334	1333	1 4	131111	3 4211

Intro
| F | C/F | Bbsus4 | Bb | |

Verse 1

F   C/F
Waking stream of con - sciousness

        G/F   Bbsus4 Bb
On a sleeping street of dreams.

F   C/F
Thoughts like scattered leaves

        G/F   Bbsus4 Bb
Slowed in mid fall into the streams

Chorus 1

        Gm7 F/G   Gm7   F
Of fast ____   running rivers of choice and ____ chance.

        Gm7
And time stops here on the Delta

                        F   Bbsus4   Bb
While they dance, ____ while they ____ dance.

| *Interlude* | \|F   \|C/F   \|G/F   \|B♭sus4   B♭   \| |

Verse 2

                     F   **C/F**
I love the child ___ who steers this riverboat

              G/F   **B♭sus4 B♭**
But lately he' s crazy for the deep.

                F   **C/F**
The river seems dreamlike in the day - time

              G/F   **B♭sus4 B♭**
Someone keeps thinking in my sleep

Chorus 2   *Repeat Chorus 1*

Outro

                 F C/F   **B♭sus4**   **B♭**
While they dance, ____ while they ___ dance.

                    F C/F   **B♭sus4**   **B♭**
‖: While they dance, ___   while they ___ dance.   :‖

           F   B♭/F   F   B♭/F   F   G/F   F
Ah, do, do, do.

Fair Game

Words and Music by
Stephen Stills

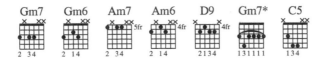

Intro

‖: Gm7 Gm6 Gm7 Gm6 Gm7 |

| Am7 Am6 Am7 Am6 Am7 :‖

‖: Gm7   Gm6   Gm7 | Am7   D9   :‖

Verse 1

Gm7   Gm6 Gm7   Gm6 Gm7
Take a look a -   round you.

Am7   D9
Tell me if you see

 Gm7   Gm6 Gm7   Gm6   Gm7
A girl who thinks she's ordinary looking.

Am7   D9
She has got the key.

Gm7   Gm6 Gm7   Gm6 Gm7
If you can get   close enough

  Am7   D9
To look into her eyes,

    Gm7   Gm6 Gm7   Gm6 Gm7
There's something spec - ial   right behind

  Am7   D9
The bitterness she hides.

GUITAR CHORD SONGBOOK

Chorus 1	**Gm7***
	And you're fair ____ game.
	C5
	You never know what she'll decide.
	Gm7*
	You're fair ____ game.
	C5
	Just relax, enjoy the ride.
Interlude 1	‖: Gm7 Gm6 Gm7 Gm6 Gm7 ‖
	| Am7 Am6 Am7 Am6 Am7 :‖

Verse 2

Gm7   Gm6 Gm7   Gm6 Gm7
Find a way to   reach her.

Am7   D9
Make yourself a fool.

**   Gm7   Gm6 Gm7   Gm6 Gm7**
But, do it with a   lit - tle class,

Am7   D9
Disregard the rules.

**   Gm7   Gm6 Gm7   Gm6 Gm7**
'Cause this one knows the   bottom line,

Am7   D9
Couldn't get a date.

**   Gm7   Gm6 Gm7   Gm6 Gm7**
The ugly duck - ling   striking back,

Am7   D9
She'll decide her fate.

Chorus 2   *Repeat Chorus 1*

Interlude 2   *Repeat Interlude 1*

	Gm7 **Gm6 Gm7**
Verse 3	The ones you nev - er notice

    Gm6 Gm7   Am7   D9
        Are the ones you have to watch.

      Gm7   Gm6 Gm7
    She's pleasant and she's friendly,

    Gm6 Gm7   Am7   D9
        While she's looking at your crotch.

      Gm7   Gm6 Gm7   Gm6 Gm7
    An' try your hand at   conver - sa - tion.

    Am7   D9
    Gossip is a lie.

      Gm7   Gm6 Gm7   Gm6 Gm7
    And sure enough, she'll take you home,

      Am7   D9
    And make you wanna die.

Chorus 3	*Repeat Chorus 1*
Interlude 3	*Repeat Interlude 1*

Guitar Solo
‖: Gm7 Gm6 Gm7 Gm6 Gm7 | Am7   D9   :‖ *Play 4 times*
‖: Gm7* | C5   :‖

Outro
‖: Gm7 Gm6 Gm7 Gm6 Gm7 |
| Am7 Am6 Am7 Am6 Am7 :‖
| Gm7 Gm6 Gm7   ‖

Got It Made

Words and Music by
Stephen Stills and Neil Young

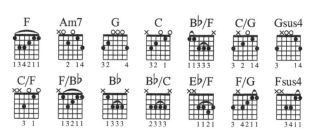

Intro

‖: F Am7 G │   │ F Am7 G │   :‖

Verse 1

    C   G
You know you are a friend of mine.

F   G
Babe, you been gone an aw - ful long time.

C   G
You might re - member me,

F   G
I tried to set your soul ___ free.

Chorus 1

N.C.   F   Am7 G
    Glad that you got it made.

               F   Am7   G
When did you finalize ___ your last trade?

             F   Am7 G
You are the only one

           F   Bb/F   G   C/G
I've ever seen do what you done, done.

F   Bb/F   G   C/G
Anything that you done, done.

F   Bb/F
You are the only one

G   C/G
Don't put me under your gun.

Interlude 1 |F Am7 G | |F Am7 G |
                 | |F Am7 G | |

Verse 2
```
C                 G         Gsus4
  I'm gonna be miss - ing you
```
```
F         Bb/F      G           C/G      G
Even though I understand that you're not ____ through.
```
```
C         G         C/F
  Go on, take it day by day.
```
```
F                   G
Seems like I lost you an - yway.
```

Chorus 2
```
N.C.           F         Am7  G
Glad that you got it made.
```
```
               F     Am7       G
When did you finalize ____ your last trade?
```
```
               F     Am7  G
You are the only one
```
```
               F       Bb/F        G    C/G
That I've ever seen do what you done, done.
```
```
F         Bb/F      G     C/G
Anything that you done, done.
```
```
F           Bb/F
You are the only one.
```
```
G         C/G
Don't put me under your gun.
```

Interlude 2 ||: F Am7 G | |F Am7 G | :||

Bridge
```
F/Bb      Bb      Bb/C    C
When you came to save the world,
```
```
 Eb/F        F           F/G  G
I caused your dreams to fade.
```
```
F/Bb      Bb   Bb/C     C
I couldn't do  what you did,
```
```
  Fsus4      F           G
And rained on ____ your parade.
```

                             F   **Am7 G**

Interlude 3   Glad that you got it made.

               | **F   Am7 G** | | **F Am7 G** | |

             F Am7 G   **F**   **Am7 G**

                   (Glad that you got it made.)

                     F   **Am7 G**   **F Am7 G**

            Hard set of changes ____ for anyone that I know.

                   F   **Am7**   **G**

            You're gon - na make it, make it, make it,

                    F   **Am7**   **G**

            Better for you ____ and me and anyone else you know.

            F Am7   **G**

                Just don't forget me.

            F Am7 G   **F Am7 G**

                I'll be there when you're done.

                    F   **Am7 G**

            (Glad that you got it made.)

                    F   **Am7**   **G**   **F**

            And in the meantime, meantime, ____ you'll get to know yourself.

                  Am7   **G**   **F Am7 G**

            So don't judge ____ anyone ____ else, anyone.

             F Am7 G

            No.

            C   **G**

Verse 3   It doesn't matter, I don't mind.

            F   **G**   **C/G**   **G**

            I know that you'll re - member some - time.

            C   **G**   **F**   **G**

              Even if you never do, all you need to worry 'bout now is you.

Chorus 3   *Repeat Chorus 2*

Interlude 4   *Repeat Interlude 2*

            F Am7 G   **F**   **Am7 G**

Outro   ‖:   Glad that you got it made.   :‖ ***Repeat and fade***

Guinnevere

Words and Music by
David Crosby

Open Em11 tuning::
(low to high) E-B-D-G-A-D

Melody:

Guin-ne-vere _____

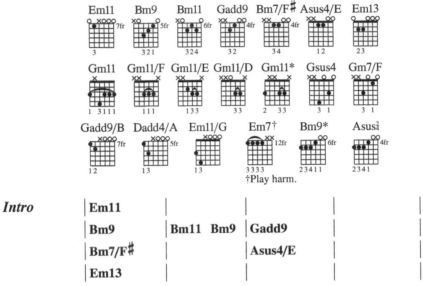

Em11   Bm9   Bm11   Gadd9   Bm7/F♯   Asus4/E   Em13

Gm11   Gm11/F   Gm11/E   Gm11/D   Gm11*   Gsus4   Gm7/F

Gadd9/B   Dadd4/A   Em11/G   Em7†   Bm9*   Asus⁴₂

†Play harm.

Intro

| Em11 | | | | |

| Bm9 | Bm11 Bm9 | Gadd9 | |

| Bm7/F♯ | | Asus4/E | |

| Em13 | | | |

Verse 1

Em13
Guinnevere had green eyes like yours, milady, like yours.

Gm11 Gm11/F   Gm11/E
She'd walk down through the garden

    Gm11/D   Gm11* Em13
In the morning after   it   rained.

Gsus4   Gm7/F
Peacocks wandered aimlessly

Gsus4   Gm7/F Gadd9/B Dadd4/A Em11/G Em13
Underneath an orange tree.

Gadd9/B Dadd4/A Em11/G   Em13
         Why can't ___ she see me?

| ¾ Gadd9/B Dadd4/A | ⁴⁄₄ Em11/G Em13 | Em7 | |

| Em13 | | | |

Verse 2

Em13
    Guinnivere drew pentagrams like yours, milady, like yours.

Gm11   Gm11/F   Gm11/E
   Late at night, when she thought

     Gm11/D   Gm11* Em13
That no one was watching ___ at ___ all, on the wall.

 Gsus4   Gm7/F
(Do, do, do, do.) Do, do, do, do,

Gsus4   Gm7/F Gadd9/B Dadd4/A Em11/G Em13
Do, do, do, do, do, do, do.

Gadd9/B Dadd4/A Em11/G Em13
  She shall ___ be free.

| $\frac{3}{4}$ Gadd9/B Dadd4/A | $\frac{4}{4}$ Em11/G Em13 | Em7 | | |

Bridge

Bm9*   A7sus$\frac{2}{4}$ Bm9*
  As she turns her gaze,   down the slope to the har - bor

       Em13
Where I lay ___ anchored for a day.

Verse 3

Em13
    Guinnivere had golden hair like yours, milady, like yours.

Gm11   Gm11/F   Gm11/E
   Streaming out when we'd ride

        Gm11/D   Gm11* Em13
Through the warm wind down by ___ the ___ bay yesterday.

Gsus4   Gm7/F
Seagulls circle endlessly,

  Gsus4   Gm7/F Gadd9/B Dadd4/A Em11/G Em13
I   sing in silent harmony.

Gadd9/B Dadd4/A Em11/G Em13
     We shall be free.

| $\frac{3}{4}$ Gadd9/B Dadd4/A | $\frac{4}{4}$ Em11/G Em13 | Em7 | | |

Outro

Em11				
Bm9 Bm11	Bm9	Gadd9		
Bm7/F♯		Asus4/E		
‖: Em13		:‖ *Repeat and fade*	

Helplessly Hoping

Words and Music by
Stephen Stills

Melody:

Help - less - ly hop - ing __ her __ har - le-quin

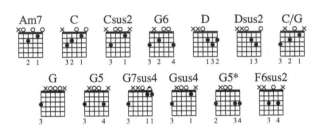

Am7   C   Csus2   G6   D   Dsus2   C/G

G   G5   G7sus4   Gsus4   G5*   F6sus2

Intro | Am7 | C Csus2 C | G6 | D Dsus2 D Dsus2 |

Verse 1
    Am7   C   C/G Csus2   G
Helplessly hoping her har - lequin hovers near - by,

C/G   G C/G D   Dsus2 D Dsus2
  Await - ing a word.

Am7   Csus2
Gasping at the glimpses of gentle true spirit,

  G C/G G   C/G   D Dsus2
He runs,   wishing he could fly,

D   Am7   Csus2   G C/G G C/G D Dsus2 D Dsus2
Only to trip at the sound ___ of goodbye.

Verse 2
    Am7   C C/G Csus2
Wordlessly watching, he waits by the win - dow

        G   C/G   G   C/G   D Dsus2 D Dsus2
And won - ders ___ at the empty place inside.

Am7   Csus2   G
Heartlessly helping him - self to her bad dreams, he wor - ries.

C/G   G   C/G   D Dsus2 D
  Did he ___ hear ___ a good - bye

    Am7 Csus2 G G5
Or even   hello?

G7sus4 G5   G   Gsus4
They are one ___ per - son.

          G5*   Gsus4
They are two, ___ a - lone.

          G5*   Gsus4
They are three ___ togeth - er.

        G5* F6sus2   Csus2 G C/G G C/G G
They are for _____ each other.

Verse 3

Am7   C   C/G   Csus2
Stand by the stairway, you'll see some - thing certain

      G   C/G   G   C/G   D Dsus2 D Dsus2
To tell ___ you ___ confu - sion has its cost.

Am7   Csus2   G
Love isn't lying, it's loose ___ in a lady who lin - gers

C/G G   C/G   D Dsus2
    Saying she is lo - st

D   Am7   Csus2   G G5
  And choking   on hello.

Chorus 2

G7sus4 G5   G5*   G7sus4
They are one ___ per - son.

     G   G5*   G7sus4
They are two, ___ a - lone.

        G   G5*   G7sus4
They are ___ three ___ to - gether.

          G5* F6sus2 Csus2 C Csus2 G C/G G C/G G
They are for _____ each other.

Immigration Man

Words and Music by
Graham Nash

Melody:

There I was at the im-mi-gra-tion scene,

Drop D tuning:
(low to high) D-A-D-G-B-E

Dadd9   C/D   Bb6(add4)/D

Intro |Dadd9 |C/D | |Bb6(add4)/D |

                 Dadd9   C/D

Verse 1   There I was at the immigration scene,

                                   Bb6(add4)/D

          Shinin' and feelin' clean, could it be a sin?

                 Dadd9   C/D

          I got stopped by the immigration man,

                                 Bb6(add4)/D

          He said he doesn't know if he can let me in.

                 Dadd9   C/D

Chorus 1   Let me in, ____ Immigra - tion Man.

                         Bb6(add4)/D

          Can I cross the line and pray I can stay another day?

                 Dadd9   C/D

          Let me in, ____ Immigra - tion Man.

                           Bb6(add4)/D   Dadd9 C/D Dadd9

          I won't toe your line today, I can't see it anyway, hey.

	Dadd9 **C/D**
Verse 2	There he was with his immigration face,

                                          B♭6(add4)/D
Givin' me a paper chase, but the sun was comin'

         Dadd9   **C/D**
'Cause all at once ___ he looked into my ___ space

                                             B♭6(add4)/D
Stamped a number over my face, and he sent me runnin'.

                    Dadd9   **C/D**
Chorus 2   Won't you let me in, ___ Immigra - tion Man?

                          B♭6(add4)/D
Can I cross the line and pray I can stay another day?

                    Dadd9   **C/D**
Won't you let me in, ___ Immigra - tion Man?

                          B♭6(add4)/D
I won't toe your line today, I can't see it anyway.

             Dadd9   **C/D**
Verse 3   Here I am with my immigration form.

                                          B♭6(add4)/D
It's big enough to keep me warm when a cold wind's comin'.

                    Dadd9   **C/D**
So go where you will, ___ as long as you think you can.

You'd better watch out, watch out for the man

             B♭6(add4)/D
Anywhere you're goin'.

                    Dadd9   **C/D**
Chorus 3   Come on and let me in, ___ Immigra - tion Man.

                          B♭6(add4)/D
Can I cross the line and pray? Take your fin - gers from the tray.

             Dadd9   **C/D**
Let me in, ___ Irrita - tion Man.

                    B♭6(add4)/D
I won't toe your line today, I can't see it anyway.

Outro   ‖: **Dadd9** │**C/D**   │   │ **Dadd9** :‖ *Repeat and fade*

In My Dreams

Words and Music by
David Crosby

Melody:

Look at those _ dan - cers glid - in' a - round. _

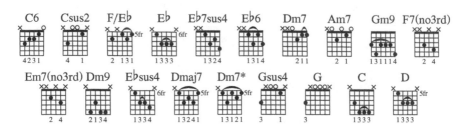

| C6 | Csus2 | F/E♭ | E♭ | E♭7sus4 | E♭6 | Dm7 | Am7 | Gm9 | F7(no3rd) |

| Em7(no3rd) | Dm9 | E♭sus4 | Dmaj7 | Dm7* | Gsus4 | G | C | D |

Intro   ‖: C6 Csus2 │ C6 Csus2 :‖

            C6   Csus2   C6   Csus2
Verse 1   Look at those ____ dancers glid - in' a - round.

            C6   Csus2   C6 Csus2
              Seems as if their feet   don't hardly

            F/E♭   E♭   E♭7sus4 E♭6
            Touch the ground.

            C6   Csus2   C6   Csus2
            Look at them smiling like they   knew one another

                    C6   Csus2 C6   Csus2
            And they   never _____   would

            F/E♭ E♭   E♭7sus4 E♭6
            Come down.

                    Dm7   Am7
            Turn a - round, and hold me.

                    Gm9
            I'd like to see your face alone.

                    N.C.(F7(no3rd)) (E7(no3rd)) Dm7   Dm9
            I'm hoping there's   someone   home,

Verse 2

C6   Csus2   C6   Csus2
I'd like to meet ya.   Who do you see?

C6   Csus2   C6   Csus2
Introduce yourself to whichever of ____ me

        F/E♭ E♭ E♭sus4 E♭
Is near -   by.

C6   Csus2   C6   Csus2
Close behind your eyes, laugh - ing at me,

       C6   Csus2   C6 Csus2
And I'm stuck with no instructions that I can ___ see

        F/E♭ E♭ E♭7sus4 E♭6
To steer ____ by.

       Dm7   Am7
Stick a - round, its tricky ground.

       Gm9
I'd like to see your face alone.

      N.C.(F7(no3rd)) (Em7(no3rd)) Dm7   Dm9
I'm hoping there's someone   home.

Verse 3

C6   Csus2   C6   Csus2
Two or three ___ people fad - ing in and out,

       C6 Csus2   C6   Csus2
Like a ra - dio ___ station I'm thinking a - bout

       F/E♭ E♭ E♭sus4 E♭
But I can't ____ hear.

C6   Csus2   C6   Csus2
Who gets ___ breakfast? Who ___ gets the lunch?

C6   Csus2 C6   Csus2
  Who gets to be the boss of this ___ bunch?

       F/E♭   E♭ E♭sus4 E♭
Who will ___ steer?

   Dm7 Am7   Gm9
Turn - ing, turning, to see your face alone.

      N.C.(F7(no3rd)) (Em7(no3rd)) Dm7   Dm9
I'm hoping there's someone   home.

Bridge

Dmaj7 Dm7*
Dream, do you dream?

Gsus4 G Gsus4 G C D   C D
Dream - ing,   do ___ you?

Dmaj7   Dm7*
  Dream, do you dream?

Gsus4 G Gsus4 G C D   C
Dream - ing,   do ___ you?

Outro

  Dm7
‖: In my dreams I can see, I can.

     G
I can see a love that could be. ‖ *Repeat and fade*

It Doesn't Matter

Words and Music by
Stephen Stills and Chris Hillman

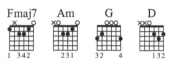

Intro |Fmaj7 | |Am | |

Verse 1

Fmaj7   Am
Fallin' and spinnin', losin' and winnin', keep - in' my head.

Fmaj7   Am
Watchin' for signals, wearisome vigil, was ___ I misled?

          G   D
I remem - ber you said that you don't want to forget me.

Fmaj7   G   Am Fmaj7 Am
It doesn't matter which of our fantasies fled.

Verse 2

Fmaj7   Am
Ev'ry tomorrow lookin' to borrow a piece of today.

Fmaj7   Am
Run a bit faster, here comes the catcher mak - in' his play,

          G   D
You had bet - ter not stay, you will soon be surrounded.

Fmaj7   G   Am
It doesn't matter which of our fantasies stay.

Guitar Solo   *Repeat Verse 2 (Instrumental)*

Verse 3

Fmaj7   Am
Lonely and winsome, calling for someone liv - ing right now.

Fmaj7   Am
Something is shallow, ugly and hollow, doesn't even allow you

          G   D
To want ___ to know how you might live for the living

And give for the giving moment by moment, one day at a time.

Fmaj7   G   Am
It doesn't matter, it's nothing but dreaming an - yhow.

Just a Song Before I Go

Words and Music by
Graham Nash

Melody:

Just a song — be - fore — I go —

(Capo 2nd fret)

Em7	Bm7	C	Am7	Em9	G	F	Bm(add4)	Esus$\frac{2}{4}$
12 4	13121	32 1	2 1	13 2	3 4	134211	342	142

Intro

‖: Em7 | Bm7 | C | Am7 :‖

Verse 1

Em9   Bm7   C   Am7
Just a song before ____ I go to whom it may concern.

Em9   Bm7   C   Am7
Traveling twice the speed ____ of sound, it's easy to get burned.

G   F   Am7   Bm(add4)
When the shows were o - ver, we had to get back home.

  G   F   Am7
And when we opened up the door, I had to be alone.

Verse 2

    Em9   Bm7   C   Am7
She helped me with my suit - case, she stands before my eyes.

Em9   Bm7   C   Am7
Driving me to the air - port and to the friendly skies.

G   F Am7   Bm(add4)
Going through secu - rity, I held her for so long.

  G   F   Am7
She fin'lly looked at me in love, and she was gone.

Guitar Solo

‖: Em9 | Bm7 | C | Am7 :‖

Outro-Verse

Em9   Bm7   C   Am7
Just a song before ____ I go, a lesson to be learned.

Em9   Bm7   C   Esus$\frac{2}{4}$
Traveling twice the speed ____ of sound, it's easy to get burned.

Love the One You're With

Words and Music by
Stephen Stills

Open E5 tuning, down 2 steps:
(low to high) C–C♭–C–C♭–G–C

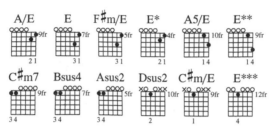

| A/E | E | F♯m/E | E* | A5/E | E** |
| C♯m7 | Bsus4 | Asus2 | Dsus2 | C♯m/E | E*** |

Intro | A/E   E | F♯m/E   E* | A/E   E | A5/E   E** |

Verse 1

           A/E   E   F♯m/E   E*
If you're down ____   and confused,

           A/E   E   F♯m/E   E*
And you don't remem - ber   who you're talkin' to.

           A/E   E   F♯m/E   E*
Concentra-tion   slip away,

           A/E   E   F♯m/E   E*
'Cause your ba - by   is so far away.

Pre-Chorus 1

                 C♯m7   Bsus4   Asus2
Well, there's a rose ____   in the fisted glove

          C♯m7   Bsus4   Asus2
And the ea - gle flies   with the dove.

          C♯m7   Bsus4   Asus2
And if you can't ____ be   with the one you love, honey,

Love the one you're with.

Chorus 1

```
A/E  E                      F#m/E  E*
    Love the one you're with.        Love the one you're with.

A/E  E                      F#m/E  E*
    Love the one you're with.
```

Verse 2

```
E*          A/E  E          F#m/E  E*
  Don't be an-gry,   don't be sad,

        A/E   E                  F#m/E      E*
And don't sit cryin'   over good times ___ you had.

        A/E  E              F#m/E  E*
There's a girl    right next to you

            A/E   E                  F#m/E  E*
And she's just waitin'   for somethin' to do.
```

Pre-Chorus 2

```
E*                C#m7  Bsus4        Asus2
And there's a rose ___          in the fisted glove

        C#m7        Bsus4        Asus2
And the ea - gle flies      with the dove.

            C#m7  Bsus4            Asus2
And if you can't ___ be      with the one you love, honey,


Love the one you're with.
```

Chorus 2

```
A/E  E                      F#m/E  E*
    Love the one you're with.        Love the one you're with.
```

Bridge

Dsus2 C#m/E Dsus2 C#m/E
‖: Do,   do,   do,   do,

Dsus2 C#m/E E***
Do,   do,   do, do. :‖ *Play 3 times*

E   N.C.
Do, do, do, do, do, do.

Organ Solo

| C#m7 Bsus4 | Asus2 | C#m7 Bsus4 | Asus2

| C#m7 Bsus4 | Asus2
                        Love the one you're with.

Chorus 3   *Repeat Chorus 1*

Verse 3

E*   A/E E   F#m/E E*
   Turn your heart-ache   right into joy.

            A/E E   F#m/E E*
She's a girl, ___   and you're a boy.

            A/E E   F#m/E E*
Get it togeth - er,   make it nice.

     A/E   E   F#m/E E*
Ain't gonna   need any more advice.

Pre-Chorus 3   *Repeat Pre-Chorus 2*

Chorus 4

A/E   E   F#m/E E*
   Love the one you're with.   Love the one you're with.

A/E   E   F#m/E E*
   Love the one you're with.

Outro   *Repeat Bridge*

Lady of the Island

Words and Music by
Graham Nash

Hold-ing you close, un-dis-turbed, __ be-fore __ the fire. __

Tuning:
(low to high) Eb-Bb-F-G-Bb-Eb

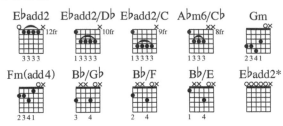

Verse 1

     Ebadd2   **Ebadd2/Db**
Holding you close, undisturbed, before ___ the fire.

    Ebadd2/C   **Abm6/Cb**
The pressure in my chest when you breathe in my ear.

   Gm   **Fm(add4)**
We both knew this would happen when you first appeared.

 Gm   **Fm(add4)**
My Lady of ___ the Island.

Verse 2

    Ebadd2   **Ebadd2/Db**
The brownness of your body in the fire ___ glow

    Ebadd2/C   **Abm6/Cb**
Ex - cept the places where the sun re - fused to go.

   Gm   **Fm(add4)**
Our bodies were a perfect fit   in afterglow

    Gm   **Fm(add4)**
We lay, ___ my Lady of ___ the Island.

Bridge

Bb/Gb   Bb/F   Bb/E   Ebadd2*
Letting myself wander through the world ___ inside your eyes.

Bb/Gb   Bb/F   Bb/E   Ebadd2
You know I'd like to stay ___ here until ev - 'ry tear runs dry.

Verse 3

Ebadd2/Db   Ebadd2/C
Do, do, do, do, do, do, do, do, do,

                    Abm6/Cb
Do, do, do, do, do, do, do, do, ___ do, do, do, do, do, do,

Gm   Fm(add4)
Do, do, do, do, do, do, do, ___ do, do,

    Gm   Fm(add4)
Do, do, ___ do, do, do, do, do, do, do, ___ do,

Gm   Fm(add4)
My La - dy of the Island.

Verse 4

Ebadd2   Ebadd2/Db
Wrapped around each other in the peep - ing sun.

Ebadd2/C   Abm6/Cb
Beams of sunshine light the stage, the red lights on.

  Gm   Fm(add4)   Gm
I never want to finish what I've just begun with you

    Fm(add4)
My Lady of ___ the Island.

Outro

Gm   Fm(add4)
Do, do, do, do, do, do, do, do,

            Gm   Fm(add4)
Do, do, do, do, do, do, do, do, ___ do, do,

     Ebadd2*
Do, do, do, do, do, do, do, do.

rrakesh Express

is and Music by
nam Nash

Melody:

Look - in' at _____ the world _

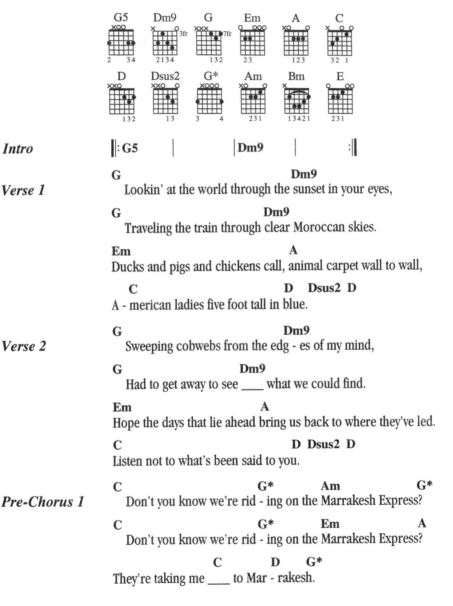

G5 Dm9 G Em A C

D Dsus2 G* Am Bm E

Intro

‖: G5 | | Dm9 | :‖

Verse 1

G   Dm9
   Lookin' at the world through the sunset in your eyes,

G   Dm9
   Traveling the train through clear Moroccan skies.

Em   A
Ducks and pigs and chickens call, animal carpet wall to wall,

  C   D   Dsus2 D
A - merican ladies five foot tall in blue.

Verse 2

G   Dm9
   Sweeping cobwebs from the edg - es of my mind,

G   Dm9
   Had to get away to see ___ what we could find.

Em   A
Hope the days that lie ahead bring us back to where they've led.

C   D Dsus2 D
Listen not to what's been said to you.

Pre-Chorus 1

C   G*   Am   G*
   Don't you know we're rid - ing on the Marrakesh Express?

C   G*   Em   A
   Don't you know we're rid - ing on the Marrakesh Express?

               C   D   G*
They're taking me ___ to Mar - rakesh.

Chorus 1

                              G
All aboard ___ that train.

All aboard that train.

Bridge

  Bm   G5
I've been savin' all my money just to take you there.

  E   C
I smell the garden in your hair.

Verse 3

  G   Dm9
Take the train from Casablan - ca going south,

  G   Dm9
Blowing smoke rings from the cor - ners of my mouth.

Em   A
Colored cottons hang in the air, charming cobras in the square,

C   D
Striped djellebas we can wear at home.

           Dsus2   D
Well, let me hear you, now.

Pre-Chorus 2

  C   G*   Am   G*
Don't you know we're rid - ing on the Marrakesh Express?

  C   G*   Em   A
Don't you know we're rid - ing on the Marrakesh Express?

              C   D   G*
They're taking me ___ to Mar - rakesh.

  C   G*   Am   G*
Don't you know we're rid - ing on the Marrakesh Express?

  C   G*   Em   A
Don't you know we're rid - ing on the Marrakesh Express?

              C   D   G*
They're taking me ___ to Mar - rakesh.

Chorus 2

                              G
All aboard ___ that train.

All aboard that train.

          Dm9
All aboard.

Outro   ‖: Dm9 | | | :‖ *Repeat and fade*

ilitary Madness

ords and Music by
raham Nash

Melody:

In an up - stairs room __ in Black - pool,

C   Am   F

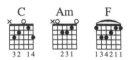

32 14   2 3 1   1 3 4 2 1 1

Intro

| C | | | | | | |

| Am | | | C | | | |

| Am | | | |

Verse 1

C   Am
In an upstairs room in Blackpool,   by the side of a northern sea.

C   Am
The Army had my father,   and my mother was having me.

Chorus 1

F   Am   F   Am
Milit'ry mad - ness   was killing my coun - try.

F   Am   F   C   Am
Solit'ry sad - ness   comes over me.

Verse 2

C   Am
And after the school was over   and I moved to the other side,

C   Am
I found another country   but I never lost my pride.

```
                    F              Am    F                        Am
Chorus 2            Milit'ry mad - ness    was killing the coun - try.

                    F              Am    F              C     Am
                    Solit'ry sad - ness    creeps over me.

                    C                          Am
Verse 3             And after the wars are over    and the body count is finally filed,

                    C                          Am
                    I hope The Man discovers    what's driving the people wild.

                    F              Am    F                        Am
Chorus 3            Milit'ry mad - ness    is killing our coun - try.

                    F              Am    F                  C
                    So much sad - ness    between you and ___ me.

                    Am
                    War.

                    C      Am    C      Am
Outro               ‖: War,    war,    war,    war. :‖    Repeat and fade
```

...sic Is Love

...rds and Music by David Crosby,
...aham Nash and Neil Young

Ev-'ry-bod-y say-in'   mu-sic is   love.

DADDAD tuning down 1/2 step:
(low to high) Db-Ab-Db-Db-Ab-Db

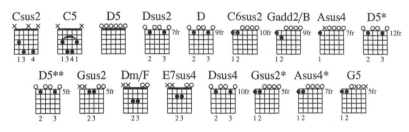

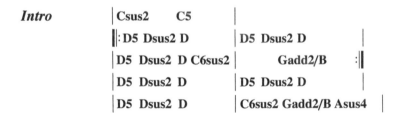

Intro

| Csus2   C5 |
:—: D5 Dsus2 D	D5 Dsus2 D
D5 Dsus2 D C6sus2	Gadd2/B :‖
D5 Dsus2 D	D5 Dsus2 D
D5 Dsus2 D	C6sus2 Gadd2/B Asus4

D5 Dsus2 D   D5 Dsus2 D D5*
Ev - 'ry - body sayin' mu - sic   is love.

D5 Dsus2 D   D5 C6sus2   Gadd2/B
Ev - 'ry - body sayin' it's,   you know it is.   Mmm.

D5 Dsus2 D   D5 Dsus2 D   D5* D5
Ev - 'ry - one, yes,   ev - 'ry - one,

      Dsus2 D   D5 C6sus2   Gadd2/B
Ev - 'ry - body sayin'   music is, mu - sic is love.

D5 Dsus2 D   D5 Dsus2 D   D5
Ev - 'ry - body sayin' that mu   -   sic   is love.

      Dsus2 D   D5 C6sus2 Gadd2/B
Ev - 'ry - body sayin' it's love,   love.

D5 Dsus2 D   D5 Dsus2 D   Dsus2 D5**
Ev - 'ry - body sayin' that mu - sic   is love.

      Dsus2 D   Dsus2 D C6sus2   Gadd2/B
Ev - 'ry - body say - in'   it's love. Sayin' it's love,   yeah.

   D5 Dsus2 D   Dsus2 D D5 Dsus2 D   Dsus2 D
‖: Ev - 'ry - body say - in'   that mu - sic   is love.

D5 Dsus2 D   Dsus2 D   C6sus2
Ev - 'ry - body say - in'   it's love,

      Gadd2/B
Sayin' it's love, yeah. :‖ *Play 4 times*

      Dsus2 D   Dsus2 D D5 Dsus2 D D5*
Ev - 'ry - body say - in'   that mu - sic   is love.

|D5 Dsus2 D Dsus2 D5 C6sus2 | Gadd2/B |

D5   Dsus2 D   D5   Dsus2 D   D5
Ev'ry - body's sayin' that mu - sic   is love.

      Dsus2 D   D5 C6sus2 Gadd2/B
Ev - 'ry - body's sayin' it's love.

CROSBY, STILLS & NASH   **59**

Instrumental

D5 Gsus2 Dm/F E7sus4	Dm/F E7sus4
D5** Dsus2 D5**	Dsus2
D5** Dsus2 D5** Dsus2 Dsus4	D Dsus2 D5**
D5** Dsus2 D5**	Dsus2
D5** Dsus2 D5 Dsus4	D Gsus2* Asus4*

Outro

D5   Dsus2   D5 Asus4*
Put on your colors and run. Come see!

                Dsus4 D Gsus2*
Everybody sayin' the music's for free.

D5   Dsus2   D5 Dsus2   D5 Dsus2
  Take off your clothes and lie   in the sun.

D5 Dsus2   Dsus4 D G5
Ev - 'rybody says the music's for fun.

Shadow Captain

Words and Music by
David Crosby and Craig Doerge

Melody:

Oh, Cap - tain. _____

Chord diagrams:

E7sus2 | A | E | Gmaj13 | F#7sus4 | E9sus4 | E* | E6/9(no3rd)/C# | D6/9(no3rd)

Amaj13/E | A6/9(no3rd) | Bm7add4 | E** | A/E | Bm/D | Dsus2 | E+ | F#m

G#m | Bsus4 | Gmaj7 | F#m7 | E/B | B | Em7 | F#m* | D/G | Em/A

D | Cmaj7 | D* | C#m7 | A13sus4 | Gmaj9 | C#m/F# | D#m/G# | D#7sus4

Intro

‖: E7sus2 | | | :‖

Verse 1

E7sus2
Oh, Cap - tain. What are we hiding from?

       A   E
You've been hiding from the start.

       A   E
Did some lover steal your heart,

       Gmaj13   F#7sus4
Or did the full ___ moon make you mad?

Verse 2

E9sus4
Oh, Cap - tain. Why these speechless seas

       A   E
That never come to land?

       A   E
Oh, I need to understand.

       Gmaj13   F#7sus4
Could a little light ___ be that bad?

‖:E*   :‖ *Play 6 times*

|Eᵇ(no3rd)/C♯ Dᵇ(no3rd) Amaj13/E Aᵇ(no3rd) |

|Bm7add4   E |

Bridge 1

        E**   A/E   E**
I can see your hands are roughened by the wheel and the rope.

        A/E   E**
I'd like to look to you for hope.

          Bm/D A Dsus2
I think it's hid - ing there.

     E   E+   E
This boat is blacked out like the city

        F♯m   G♯m
Awaiting bombers in the night.

        A   Bsus4
Oh, you hold your helm so tight

          Gmaj7   F♯m7
And yet the sky ___ seems so fair.

Verse 3

E/B   B   E/B   B
Who guides this ship dream - ing through the seas,

A   E   A   E
Turn - ing and search - ing

      Em7 F♯m* D/G Em/A
Which - ever way   you   please?

Verse 4

E/B   B   E/B B
  Speak to me. I need to see your face,

A   E   A   E   A E
Shad - owy Cap - tain

Em7 F♯m* D   Cmaj7
In a   dark - ened space.

Interlude 2   *Repeat Interlude 1*

| | **E****   **A/E**
| *Verse 5* | If I were to spy a city floating just above the sea,
| | **E****   **D***   **C#m7**
| | Could we stop and look for me

                               A13sus4
Among those playing on the pier?

                             E**   **A/E**
Or would you turn away, knowing it was still a ways away?

E**   **A/E**
  And if I ___ was there today,

E**   **Gmaj9**   **F#m7**
  You could not see me all that clear.

Verse 6   *Repeat Verse 3*

Verse 7   *Repeat Verse 4*

Interlude 3   *Interlude 1*

Bridge 2

     C#m/F# D#m/G# C#m/F# D#m/G#
Oh, Shadow   Captain

     C#m/F# D#m/G# C#m/F# D#m/G#
Of a charcoal ship.

C#m/F# D#m/G# C#m/F# D#m/G#
Shadow   Captain

     C#m/F# D#m/G# C#m/F# D#m/G#
Of a charcoal ship.

C#m/F# N.C.   **D#7sus4**
Trying to give the light the slip.

Outro

‖: **E***   :‖ *Play 6 times*
| **E§(no3rd)/C# D§(no3rd) Amaj13/E A§(no3rd)** |
| **Bm7add4 E** ‖

---

r House

.ds and Music by
aham Nash

Melody:

I'll   light the fire, _   you'll place the flow - ers

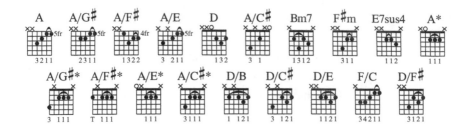

A   A/G♯   A/F♯   A/E   D   A/C♯   Bm7   F♯m   E7sus4   A*

A/G♯*   A/F♯*   A/E*   A/C♯*   D/B   D/C♯   D/E   F/C   D/F♯

Verse 1

    A   A/G♯
I'll light the fire,

A/F♯   A/E
You'll place the flow - ers

          D   A/C♯   Bm7 F♯m E7sus4
In the vase ___ that you bought ___ today.

A*   A/G♯*
Staring at the fire

  A/F♯*   A/E*
For ho - urs and ho - urs

     D   A/C♯* D/B D/C♯ D/E D/C♯
While I listen to you   play your love songs

D/B D/C♯ D/E D/C♯ A* A/G♯*
All   night long for   me,

A/F♯*   A/E* D F/C
Only for me.

Verse 2

A*   A/G♯*
Come to me now
  A/F♯*   A/E*
And rest ___ your head for just ___ five minutes.
D A/C♯* Bm7 D/F♯ D/E
Ev'ry - thing is done.
A*   A/G♯*
Such a cozy room.
  A/F♯   A/E*
The win - dows are illu - minated
D A/C♯* D/B D/C♯ D/E D/C♯
By the evening sun - shine through them,
D/B D/C♯ D/E D/C♯ A* A/G♯*
Fier - y   gems for you,
A/F♯* A/E* D F/C
Only for you.

Chorus 1

A* A/G♯* A/F♯*   A/E*
Our house is a very, very, very fine house,
   D   A/C♯*
With two cats in the yard.
   D   A/C♯*
Life used to be so hard.
    D   A/C♯* D Bm7 D
Now ev - 'rything is eas - y 'cause of you and our...

Interlude

A* A/G♯* A/F♯*   A/E*
La, la, la, la, la, la, la, ___ la, la, la, la, ___ la, la, la, la,
D   A/C♯* Bm7 D/F♯ D/E
La, la, la, la, la, ___ la, la, la, la, la, la, la, la, la , la, la.
A* A/G♯* A/F♯*   A/E*
La, la, la, la, la, la, la, ___ la, la, la, la, ___ la, la, la, la,
D   F/C
La, la, la, la, la, ___ la, la, la.

Chorus 2 *Repeat Chorus 1*

Outro-Verse

A   A/G♯
I'll light the fire
  A/F♯   A/E
While you place the flow - ers
      D   F/C A
In the vase ___ that you bought ___ today.

re-Road Downs

Words and Music by Graham Nash

Melody:

I have kissed _ you,   so I'll miss _ you. _

A/E   E   E7(no3rd)   D   Bm   A   F#m   C#m

Intro

| A/E E | E7(no3rd) A/E | E | D | | |

Verse 1

A/E   E   E7(no3rd) A/E
   I have kissed you,   so I'll   miss you.

   E   E7(no3rd) A/E
On the road I'll be wantin'   you.

   E   E7(no3rd) A/E
But I have you,   'cause I love you

     E   E7(no3rd) A/E
And you have me 'cause you love me   too, yeah!

Guitar Solo 1

| A/E E | E7(no3rd) A/E | E | E7(no3rd) A/E |

| E | E7(no3rd) A/E | E | D |

| | |

Verse 2

A/E   E   E7(no3rd)   A/E
   Felt for - saken,   you'll a - waken

   E   E7(no3rd) A/E
To the joys of livin' hand in   glove.

   E   E7(no3rd)   A/E
And then I will,   lend you my will,

   E   E7(no3rd) A/E
And your days will be filled with   love.

Chorus 1

   Bm   A   F#m   E
Don't run, the time approach - es.

   Bm   A   F#m   E
Hotels and mid - night coach - es.

   Bm   A   F#m   E D
Be sure to hide the roach - es.

Guitar Solo 2

A/E E	E7(no3rd) A/E	E	E7(no3rd) A/E
E	E7(no3rd) A/E	E	D
	E D	C#m	A

Verse 3

A/E   E   E7(no3rd) A/E
 Felt re - jected,   as ex - pected

        E   E7(no3rd) A/E
You re - jected all the thoughts of work.

        E   E7(no3rd) A/E
So, I'll pray with   you to   stay with

        E   E7(no3rd) A/E
Me for - ever and we'll make it   work. Whoa!

Guitar Solo 3   *Repeat Guitar Solo 1*

Verse 4

A/E   E   E7(no3rd)   A/E
 Ele - vated,   you're e - lated

        E   E7(no3rd) A/E
'Cause I waited a year for   you.

        E   E7(no3rd) A/E
If you're thinkin'   what I'm thinkin'

        E   E7(no3rd) A/E
Then I'm gonna make my love to   you. Whoa!

Chorus 2   *Repeat Chorus 1*

Outro |E   D | C#m | A | |E   ‖

ee the Changes

Words and Music by
Stephen Stills

Melody:

She has seen _____ me chang - in'. __

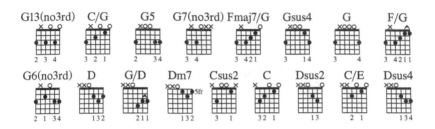

G13(no3rd) C/G G5 G7(no3rd) Fmaj7/G Gsus4 G F/G

G6(no3rd) D G/D Dm7 Csus2 C Dsus2 C/E Dsus4

Intro ‖: G13(no3rd) C/G |G5 :‖

Chorus 1

      G7(no3rd) C/G   G5
She has seen _____ me changin'.

      G7(no3rd) C/G G5
It ain't easy   rear - rangin'.

        Fmaj7/G C/G   Gsus4 G
And it gets harder   as you get old - er

      F/G   N.C.   G5   G6(no3rd) G5
And farther away   as you get closer.

Verse 1

      D G/D D   G/D D Dm7
And I   don't know the answer.

D   G/D D   G/D D Dm7
Does it   even matter?

      G   C/G G
I'm wonder - in' how.

|G5 Csus2 C |D Dsus2 D |Csus2 C Csus2 D |G C/G G |

Verse 2

G   C   D
Ten years ____ singin' right out loud.

 Csus2   Dsus2 G   C/E
I never looked, was anybody list'nin'?

G   C   D   Dsus2 D Dsus4 D
Then I fell out of a cloud.

 C   D   Dsus2   G
I hit the ground and noticed something missin'.

Chorus 2

G7(no3rd) C/G   Gsus4 G
Now _____ I have some - one

      G7(no3rd) C/G   Gsus4 G
She has seen _____ me chang - in'.

      Fmaj7/G C/G   Gsus4 G
And it gets harder   as you get old - er

  F/G   N.C.   G   C/G G
And farther away   as you get clos - er.

Verse 3

Repeat Verse 1

Verse 4

G5   C   D
Seem like something out of a dream

     C   D   G   C/E
I had years ago, yes, I remember screamin'.

G   C   D   Dsus4 D
Nobody laughing. All the good   times

     C   D   G C/G G
Gettin' harder to come ____ by without weep - in'.

Chorus 3

G7(no3rd) C/G   Gsus4 G
Now _____ I have some - one.

      G7(no3rd) C/G   Gsus4 G
She has seen _____ me chang - in'.

      Fmaj7/G C/G   Gsus4 G
And it gets harder   as you get old - er

  F/G   N.C.
And farther away.

uthbound Train

rds and Music by
aham Nash

Melody:

Lib - er - ty laugh - ing

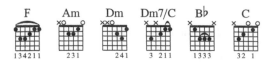

F   Am   Dm   Dm7/C   B♭   C

134211   231   241   3 211   1333   32 1

Intro

F	Am	Dm	Dm7/C Dm
B♭	C	B♭	F

Verse 1

F   Am   Dm   Dm7/C
Liberty laugh - ing and shak - ing your head.

Dm   B♭   F   Am
Can you carry the torch that'll bring home the dead

F   Am
To the land of their fa - thers

Dm   Dm7/C
Whose lives ___ you have led

Dm   B♭   F   Am
To the station at the edge of the town

B♭   C   B♭ F
On the southbound train going down?

Harmonica Solo 1   *Repeat Verse 1 (Instrumental)*

Verse 2

<pre>
       F   Am   Dm   Dm7/C
E - quality qui - etly facing the fist.

Dm   Bb   F   Am
Are you angry and tired ___ that your point has been missed?

        F   Am   Dm   Dm7/C
Will you go in the back room and study the list

Dm   Bb   F   Am
Of the gamblers using the phone

        Bb   C   Bb F
On the southbound train going down?
</pre>

Harmonica Solo 2   *Repeat Verse 1 (Instrumental)*

Verse 3

<pre>
        F   Am   Dm   Dm7/C
Fra - ternity fail - ing to fight back the tears.

Dm Bb   F   Am
Will it take an e - ternity breaking all the fears?

        F   Am   Dm   Dm7/C
And what will the passenger do when he hears

Dm   Bb   F   Am
That he's already paid for the crown

        Bb   C   Bb F
On the southbound train going down?
</pre>

Outro-
Harmonica Solo   *Repeat Verse 1 (Instrumental)*

Suite: Judy Blue Eyes

Words and Music by Stephen Stills

Melody:

It's get-ting to ___ the point ___

Open E5 tuning:
(low to high) E–E–E–E–B–E

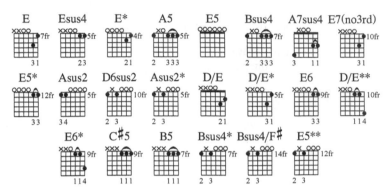

| Intro | | E | | Esus4 | E* | | | |
| | | E | | Esus4 | E* | | |

Verse 1

                          A5
It's getting to the point

                 E5   Bsus4
Where I'm no fun anymore.

          A5   A7sus4
I am sorry.

 E5   A5
   Sometimes it hurts

          E5   Bsus4
So badly I must cry out loud.

      A5   A7sus4
I am lonely.

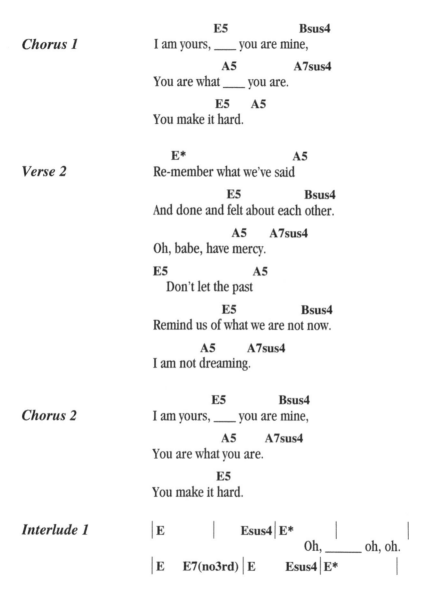

Chorus 1

                   E5   Bsus4
I am yours, ____ you are mine,

                       A5   A7sus4
You are what ____ you are.

                   E5   A5
You make it hard.

Verse 2

                E*   A5
Re-member what we've said

                   E5   Bsus4
And done and felt about each other.

                 A5   A7sus4
Oh, babe, have mercy.

E5   A5
  Don't let the past

                 E5   Bsus4
Remind us of what we are not now.

           A5   A7sus4
I am not dreaming.

Chorus 2

                   E5   Bsus4
I am yours, ____ you are mine,

                 A5   A7sus4
You are what you are.

                 E5
You make it hard.

Interlude 1

|E | Esus4|E* | |
                            Oh, _____ oh, oh.
|E   E7(no3rd)|E   Esus4|E* |

	E* A5
Verse 3	Tearing yourself

                E5   **Bsus4**
Away from me now, you are free,

          A5   **A7sus4**
And I am crying.

E5   **A5**
   This does not mean

                 E5
I don't love you, I do,

          Bsus4
That's for-ever,

          A5   **A7sus4**
Yes, and for always.

Chorus 3	*Repeat Chorus 1*

	E* A5
Verse 4	Something inside

                E5   **Bsus4**
Is telling me that I've got your secret.

          A5   **A7sus4**
Are you still list'ning?

E5   **A5**
   Fear is the lock

                E5   **Bsus4**
And laughter the key to your heart.

          A5   **A7sus4**
And I love you.

Chorus 4

         E5   Bsus4
I am yours, ___ you are mine,

           A5   A7sus4
You are what ___ you are.

        E5   A5
You make it hard.

           E5   A5
And you make it hard.

           E5   A5
And you make it hard.

           E5
And you make it hard.

Interlude 2 | E5*   Esus4 E* | E5*   Esus4 E* |

Bridge 1

E5* Esus4 E*   E5*   Esus4 E*
  Fri   -   day eve - ning,

E5* Esus4 E*   Asus2   A7sus4
  Sun-day in _____ the af - ternoon.

                      E5* Esus4 E* E5* Esus4 E*
What have you got to lose?

Bridge 2

E5* Esus4 E*   E5* Esus4 E*
  Tues   -   day morn - ing,

E5*   Esus4 E*   Asus2   A7sus4
  Please be gone, ___ I'm tired of you.

                      E5* Esus4 E* E5* Esus4 E*
What have you got to lose?

     D6sus2
Can I tell it like it is?

     Asus2*
But listen to me, baby.

D6sus2   Asus2*
  It's my heart that's a suff'rin', it's a dyin'.

                 E5* Esus4 E* E5*
That's what I have to lose.

Bridge 3

E5* Esus4 E*   E5*   Esus4 E*
I've _____ got an an - swer,

E5*   Esus4 E*Asus2   A7sus4
I'm go - ing to fly away.

                    E5* Esus4 E* E5* Esus4 E*
What have I got to lose?

Bridge 4

E5* Esus4 E*   E5*   Esus4 E*
Will _____ you come see me

E5*   Esus4   E*Asus2   A7sus4
Thurs-days and ___ Saturdays? Hey, (hey,) hey.

                   E5* Esus4 E* E5*
What have you got to lose?

Guitar Solo 1

‖: E5 | | | :‖ *Play 4 times*
| | |

Verse 5

D/E   E*
Chestnut brown canar - y,

D/E   Esus4 E*
Ruby throated spar - row,

D/E*   E   E6   E7(no3rd)
  Sing a song,   don't be long,

                D/E** E6*
Thrill me to the mar   -   row.

Guitar Solo 2

‖: E5 | | | :‖
| |

Verse 6

D/E   E*
Voices of the an - gels,

D/E   Esus4 E*
Ring around the moon - light,

D/E*   E   E6   E7(no3rd)
  Asking me, said she so free,

                D/E** E6*
"How can you catch the spar   -   row?"

Guitar Solo 3   ‖: E5 | | | :‖
| |

Verse 7

D/E   E*   Esus4 E*
Lacy, lilting lyr - ic,

D/E   Esus4 E*
Losing love, lament   -   ing,

D/E*   E   E7(no3rd)
  Change my life,   make it right,

          D/E** E6*
Be my la   -   dy.

Interlude 3

| D/E** | E6* | D/E** | E6* |
| D/E** E6* D/E**| E6* D/E**| E6* C♯5| B5 |

Outro

          N.C.
‖: Do, do, do, do, do,

Do, do, do, do, do, do.

Do, do, do, do, do,

Do, do, do, do. :‖

‖: Asus2* Bsus4* Bsus4/F♯ D6sus2   E5**   :‖ *Play 8 times*

Asus2*   Bsus4* Bsus4/F♯ D6sus2   E5**
Do, do, do, do, do,   do,   do, do, do, do, do.

Asus2*   Bsus4* Bsus4/F♯ D6sus2 E5**
Do, do, do, do, do,   do,   do,   do, do.

Asus2*   Bsus4* Bsus4/F♯ D6sus2   E5**
Do, do, do, do, do,   do,   do, do, do, do, do.

Asus2*   Bsus4* Bsus4/F♯ D6sus2 E
Do, do, do, do, do,   do,   do,   do, do.

Teach Your Children

Words and Music by
Graham Nash

Melody:

You,   who are on __ the road, __

Drop D tuning:
(low to high) D-A-D-G-B-E

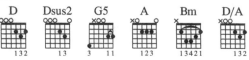

| D | Dsus2 | G5 | A | Bm | D/A |

Intro

| D Dsus2 D G5 | | D Dsus2 D | | A | |

Verse 1

D Dsus2 D   G5
You,   who are on the road,

          D Dsus2 D   A
Must have a code ___   that you can live by.

     D Dsus2 D   G5
And so,   become your - self

        D Dsus2 D   A
Because the past ___   is just a good - bye.

Chorus 1

D Dsus2 D   G5
Teach   your children well.

       D Dsus2 D   A
Their father's hell   did slowly go ___ by.

    D Dsus2 D   G5
And feed   them on your dreams.

      D Dsus2 D   A
The one they pick's   the one you'll know ___ by.

D   Dsus2 D   G5
 Don't you ev - er ask them why.

          D
If they told you, you would cry.

         Bm G5
So just look at them and sigh

A   D   Dsus2 D G5 D Dsus2 D A
 And know they love you.

Verse 2

      D **Dsus2** **D**   **G5**
And you   of ___ the tender years

                D   **Dsus2** **D**   **A**
Can't know the fears   that your elders grew ___ by.

             D   **Dsus2** **D**   **G5**
And so, please ___ help   them ___ with your ___ youth.

           D   **Dsus2** **D**   **A**
They seek the truth   before they can ___ die.

Chorus 2

D   **Dsus2** **D**   **G5**
Teach   your parents well.

           D **Dsus2** **D**   **A**
Their children's hell   will slowly go ___ by.

D   **Dsus2** **D**   **G5**
And feed   them on your dreams.

         D   **Dsus2** **D**   **A**
The one they pick's   the one you'll know ___ by.

D   **Dsus2** **D**   **G5**
Don't you ev - er ask them why.

                  D
If they told you, you would cry.

                Bm **G5**
So just look at them and sigh

A   **D**   **G5 D A D A D/A**
And know they love you.

Too Much Love to Hide

Words and Music by
Stephen Stills and Gerry Tolman

Can I sing a song to the wom - en?

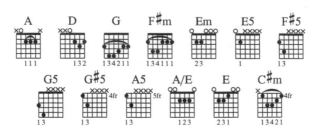

Intro	‖: A D | A :‖	*Play 4 times*

Verse 1

      A   D
Can I sing a song to the women?

      A   D
Take a look at what you might be missing.

      A   D
With a certain love that you know will stand,

      A   D
It takes a good woman and a good man, I believe.

Chorus 1

G F#m   N.C.   G   F#m N.C.   A D
I believe,   I be - lieve enough, ___   don't I?

G F#m   N.C.   Em   F#m N.C.
I believe   when I see her eyes.

G F#m   N.C.   E5   F#5 E5 G5 G#5 A5 A   D A D
I believe   there is   too much ___ love _____ to   hide.

Verse 2

      A   D
Boy, don't stand there in the shadows.

      A   D
Let her know you care about what she knows.

      A   D
Turn your mind into a win - dow,

      A   D
And the listener will lead who follows, I believe.

Chorus 2

G F#m N.C.   G   F#m N.C.   A D
I believe, I be - lieve enough, ___   don't I?

G F#m N.C.   Em   F#m N.C.
I believe   when I see her eyes.

G F#m N.C.
I believe   there is

E5   F#5 E5 G5 G#5 A5 A D A D A/E E
Too much ___ love _____ to hide.

Bridge

F#m   C#m   F#m
  If you don't trust at all, you lose.

C#m   D
You are bound to fall,

E   F#m G D A D A D
Lost behind your wall.

Guitar Solo
‖: A   D | A :‖ *Play 4 times*

Chorus 3
Repeat Chorus 1

Verse 3

     A   D
So you know now. You found out.

     A   D
This is the kind of love you can shout about.

       A   D
Leave your loneliness in the past.

     A   D
This is the kind of love that's gonna last, I believe.

Chorus 4
Repeat Chorus 1

Outro-Guitar Solo
‖: A   D | A :‖ *Repeat and fade*

Turn Back the Pages

Words and Music by
Stephen Stills and Donnie Dacus

Melody:

I thought I knew you,

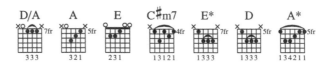

D/A A E C#m7 E* D A*

Intro

| D/A A | | D/A A | E |

Verse 1

N.C.   D/A   A   D/A   A   E
I thought I knew you,   but I did not know ___ few months a - go.

        D/A   A   C#m7
Went down the wrong road   leadin' to the past.

N.C.   D/A A D/A   A   E
I know you're try - in'   to rearrange ___ your mind,

        D/A A   C#m7
But when you're lyin',   do you laugh in my face?

Chorus 1

N.C.   E*   D A*   E*   D A*
Turn back,   turn back the pag - es.

E*   D   A*   E* D A*
Who re - members names? Who remembers fac - es?

        E* D A*   E*   D A*
Turn back,   don't drive yourself cra - zy.

E*   D   A*   E*   D A* E*
Life's too short ___ for ritu'listic chas - es.

Verse 2

N.C.   D/A   A   D/A   A   E
Maybe tomor - row,   you'll find the time ___ to cry,

        D/A   A D/A   A   C#m7
And in your sorrow   see the mir - ror never lies.

N.C.   D/A   A   D/A   A   E
Just like the last ___ time ___ you try to pull ___ me down.

        D/A   A   C#m7
You are the past time ___ and you're blind and deaf to sound.

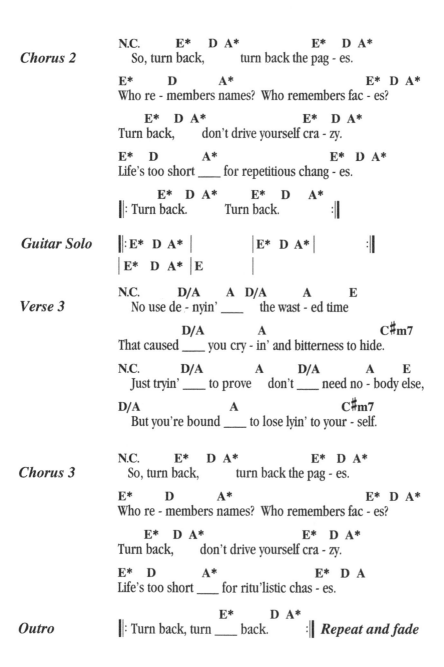

Chorus 2

N.C.   **E* D A***   **E* D A***
So, turn back,   turn back the pag - es.

E*   D   A*   **E* D A***
Who re - members names? Who remembers fac - es?

       E* D A*   **E* D A***
Turn back,   don't drive yourself cra - zy.

E* D   A*   **E* D A***
Life's too short ____ for repetitious chang - es.

      E* D A*   **E* D   A***
‖: Turn back.   Turn back.   :‖

Guitar Solo

‖: **E* D A*** | |**E* D A***| :‖
|**E* D A***|**E** |

Verse 3

N.C.   **D/A   A D/A   A   E**
No use de - nyin' ____   the wast - ed time

        D/A   A   **C#m7**
That caused ____ you cry - in' and bitterness to hide.

N.C.   **D/A   A   D/A   A   E**
Just tryin' ____ to prove don't ____ need no - body else,

D/A   **A**   **C#m7**
But you're bound ____ to lose lyin' to your - self.

Chorus 3

N.C.   **E* D A***   **E* D A***
So, turn back,   turn back the pag - es.

E*   D   A*   **E* D A***
Who re - members names? Who remembers fac - es?

       E* D A*   **E* D A***
Turn back,   don't drive yourself cra - zy.

E* D   A*   **E* D A**
Life's too short ____ for ritu'listic chas - es.

Outro

             E*   **D A***
‖: Turn back, turn ____ back.   :‖ *Repeat and fade*

Wasted on the Way

Words and Music by
Graham Nash

Melody:

Look a - round _____ me,

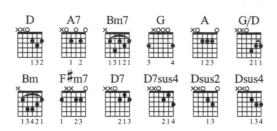

D	A7	Bm7	G	A	G/D

Bm	F#m7	D7	D7sus4	Dsus2	Dsus4

Intro | D | | | A7 | D | |

Verse 1

      D   **Bm7**
Look a - round me, I can see my life before me,

    G   **A**   **D**
Running rings around the way ____ it used to be.

               Bm7
I am older now, I have more than what I wanted,

      G   **A**   **G**   **D G/D**
But I wish that I had started long before ____ I did.

Chorus 1

D   **G**   **A**   **D**   **Bm**
  And there's so much time to make up ev'rywhere you turn,

G   **A**   **F#m7 D7 D7sus4**
Time we have wasted on the way.

G **A**   **D**   **Bm7**
So much water moving underneath the bridge.

    G   **A**   **G D**
Let the water come and carry us away.

Violin Solo

```
|D          |       |Bm7      |                   |
|G    |A    |G      |D  Dsus2  Dsus4 |
```

Verse 2

D   Bm7
    Oh, when you were young, did you question all the answers?

    G   A   G   Dsus2
Did you envy all the danc - ers who had all the nerve?

    D   Bm7
Look a - round you now, you must go for what you wanted.

    G   A   G   D
Look at all my friends who did and got what they deserved.

Chorus 2

G   A   D   Bm
So much time to make up ev'rywhere you turn,

G   A   D D7
Time we have wasted on the way.

G   A   D   Bm7
So much water moving underneath the bridge.

    G   A   D D7 D7sus4
Let the water come and carry us away.

Chorus 3

G   A   D   Bm
So much love to make up ev'rywhere you turn,

G   A   F#m7 D7 D7sus4
Love we have wasted on the way.

G   A   D   Bm7
So much water moving underneath the bridge.

    G   A   G D7
Let the water come and carry us away.

    G   A   G Dsus2 D
Let the water come and carry us away.

Wooden Ships

Words and Music by David Crosby,
Stephen Stills and Paul Kantner

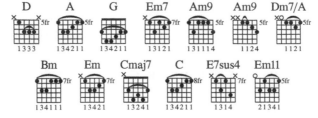

Intro

|D A G |Em7 |D A G |Em7 |

|D A G |Em7 |D A G |Em7 |

|Am9 |Em7 |Am9 |

Verse 1

            Em7   Am9   Am9#5

If you're smilin' at me, I will understand

                      Em7

'Cause that is somethin'   ev'rybody ev'rywhere

           Am9   Am9#5   Em7   Am7 Em7 Am7

Does in the   same _____ lang - uage.

Verse 2

        Em7   Am9

I can ___ see by your coat, my friend, you're from the   other side.

                Em7

There's just   one thing I got to know,

          Am7   Dm7/A   Em7 Am7 Em7 Am7

Can you tell me, please,   who won?

Verse 3

Em7

Say, can I have some of your purple berries?

Am7   Dm7/A   Em7

Yes I've been eating them for six ___ or seven weeks now.

             Am7   Dm7/A

Haven't got   sick once.

                   Em7   Am7 Dm7/A Bm A G

Prob'bly keep us both ___ alive.

Chorus 1

Em   G A D
Wooden ships on the water ver - y free and easy.

Em   G A D
Easy, you know the way it's sup - posed to be.

Em   G A D
Silver people on the shoreline, let us be.

     Cmaj7   Em C
Talkin' 'bout very free and easy.

Interlude 1

‖: E7sus4 | C   :‖ D |

Chorus 2

Em   G A D
Horror grips us as we watch you die.

Em   G A   D
All we can do is echo your an - guished cries,

Em   G A D
Stare as all human feel - ings die.

     Cmaj7   Em C
We are leaving, you don't need us.

Interlude 2

‖: Em7 | C   :‖ D |
‖: Em7 | G A D :‖ Em7 | G A D | Cmaj7 |
‖: Em7 | C   :‖ Em7 | C | D |

Chorus 3

Em   G A D
Go, take your sister, then by the hand

Em   G A D
Lead her away from this for - eign land,

Em   G A D
Far away, where we might laugh a - gain.

     Cmaj7   Em C Em C
We are leaving, you don't need _____ us.

Interlude 3

‖: Em7 | C   :‖ *Play 4 times*

Outro

Em7   C
 And it's a fair wind blowin' warm

        Em7
Out of the south over my shoulder.

C   Em7   C Em11
 Guess I'll set a course and go.

You Don't Have to Cry

Words and Music by
Stephen Stills

Melody:

In the morn - in' when _ you rise _____

Double Drop D tuning:
(low to high) D-A-D-G-B-D

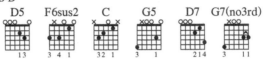

D5   F6sus2   C   G5   D7   G7(no3rd)

Intro

| D5 | | |

Verse 1

         F6sus2   **C**
In the morn - in' when you rise

      G5   **D7**
Do you think   of me and how you left me cry - in'?

      F6sus2 **C**   **G5**
Are you think - in' of telephones and managers

                D7
And where you got to be ___ at noon.

     F6sus2   **C**   **G5**
You are livin' a re - ality I left years ago

             D7
It quite nearly killed ___ me.

     F6sus2   **C**
In the long ____ run, it will make ____ you cry.

     G5   **D7**
Make you cra - zy and old before your time.

     F6sus2   **C**
And the dif - f'rence between me and you

        G5
I won't argue right ____ or wrong but I have time to

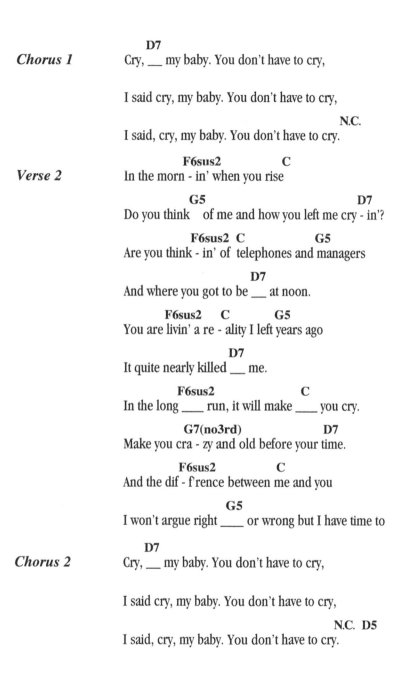

Chorus 1

       D7
Cry, __ my baby. You don't have to cry,

I said cry, my baby. You don't have to cry,

                                N.C.
I said, cry, my baby. You don't have to cry.

Verse 2

       F6sus2   **C**
In the morn - in' when you rise

       G5   **D7**
Do you think   of me and how you left me cry - in'?

       F6sus2 **C**   **G5**
Are you think - in' of telephones and managers

              D7
And where you got to be __ at noon.

       F6sus2   **C**   **G5**
You are livin' a re - ality I left years ago

           D7
It quite nearly killed __ me.

       F6sus2   **C**
In the long ___ run, it will make ___ you cry.

       G7(no3rd)   **D7**
Make you cra - zy and old before your time.

       F6sus2   **C**
And the dif - f'rence between me and you

       G5
I won't argue right ___ or wrong but I have time to

Chorus 2

       D7
Cry, __ my baby. You don't have to cry,

I said cry, my baby. You don't have to cry,

                          N.C. **D5**
I said, cry, my baby. You don't have to cry.

Southern Cross

Words and Music by Stephen Stills,
Richard Curtis and Michael Curtis

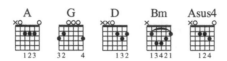

Intro |A   G |D N.C. D |A   G |D N.C. A |

Verse 1

      A   G   D   N.C. D
Got out of town ___ on a boat   goin' to southern is - lands,

      A   G   D N.C. A
Sailing a reach be - fore a following sea.

                            G   D   N.C. D
She was making for the trades ___ on the outside

      A   G   D N.C. A
And the downhill run   to Papee - te.

Verse 2

      A   G   D   N.C. D
Off the wind ___ on this heading lie the Mar - que - sas.

      A   G   D N.C.   A
We got eighty feet of a waterline nice - ly mak - ing way.

            G   D N.C. D
In a noisy bar in Avalon I tried to call you,

      A   G   D   Bm   A
But on a midnight watch I realized why twice you ran away.

Think about...

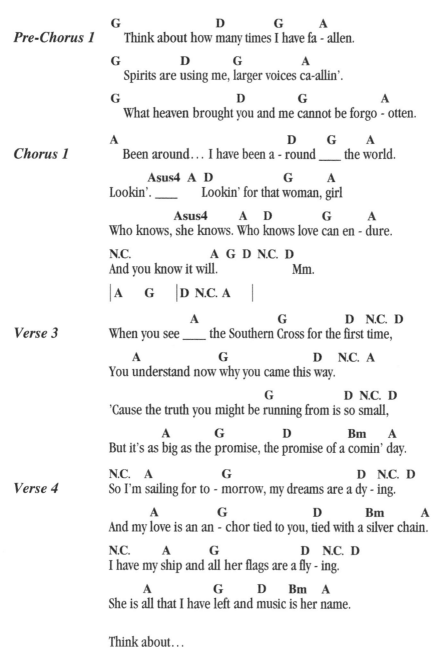

Pre-Chorus 1

G   D   G A
Think about how many times I have fa - allen.

G   D   G   A
Spirits are using me, larger voices ca-allin'.

G   D   G   A
What heaven brought you and me cannot be forgo - otten.

Chorus 1

A   D G A
Been around… I have been a - round ___ the world.

   Asus4 A D   G   A
Lookin'. ___ Lookin' for that woman, girl

    Asus4 A D   G   A
Who knows, she knows. Who knows love can en - dure.

N.C.   A G D N.C. D
And you know it will.   Mm.

|A G |D N.C. A |

Verse 3

      A   G   D N.C. D
When you see ___ the Southern Cross for the first time,

   A   G   D N.C. A
You understand now why you came this way.

          G   D N.C. D
'Cause the truth you might be running from is so small,

    A   G   D   Bm A
But it's as big as the promise, the promise of a comin' day.

Verse 4

N.C. A   G   D N.C. D
So I'm sailing for to - morrow, my dreams are a dy - ing.

   A   G   D   Bm   A
And my love is an an - chor tied to you, tied with a silver chain.

N.C. A G   D N.C. D
I have my ship and all her flags are a fly - ing.

    A   G D Bm A
She is all that I have left and music is her name.

Think about…

Pre-Chorus 2 *Repeat Pre-Chorus 1*

                        A   **D**   **G**   **A**
Chorus 2   Been around… I have been a - round ___ the world.

                            Asus4 A D   **G**   **A**
                    Lookin'. ___   Lookin' for that woman, girl

                    Asus4 A   D   **G**   **A**
                            Who knows love can en - dure.

                    N.C.   **A G D N.C. D**   **A**   **G**
                    And you know it will.   And you know ___ it will.

                    D N.C. A
                            Peace.

Interlude   ‖: **A   G** | **D N.C. D** | **A   G** | **D N.C. A** :‖

                        A   **G**   **D   N.C. D**
Verse 5   So we cheated and we lied ___ and we test - ed.

                        A   **G**   **D   N.C.   A**
                    And we never failed to fail; it was the easi - est thing to do.

                                    G   **D   N.C. D**
                    You will survive ___ being best - ed.

                                    A   **G**   **D**   **Bm   A**
                    Somebody fine ___ will come along, make me for - get about loving you

                    N.C.   **A**   **G D N.C. D**
                    And the Southern Cross.

                    | **A   G** | **D N.C. D**   ‖

Guitar Chord Songbooks

Each book includes complete lyrics, chord symbols, and guitar chord diagrams.

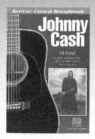 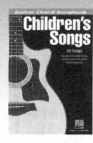  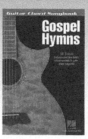 

Acoustic Hits
More than 60 songs: Against the Wind • Name • One • Southern Cross • Take Me Home, Country Roads • Teardrops on My Guitar • Who'll Stop the Rain • Ziggy Stardust • and more.
00701787 ....$14.99

Acoustic Rock
80 acoustic favorites: Blackbird • Blowin' in the Wind • Layla • Maggie May • Me and Julio down by the Schoolyard • Pink Houses • and more.
00699540.................................$21.99

Alabama
50 of Alabama's best: Angels Among Us • The Closer You Get • If You're Gonna Play in Texas (You Gotta Have a Fiddle in the Band) • Mountain Music • When We Make Love • and more.
00699914................................$14.95

The Beach Boys
59 favorites: California Girls • Don't Worry Baby • Fun, Fun, Fun • Good Vibrations • Help Me Rhonda • Wouldn't It Be Nice • dozens more!
00699566.................................$19.99

The Beatles
100 more Beatles hits: Lady Madonna • Let It Be • Ob-La-Di, Ob-La-Da • Paperback Writer • Revolution • Twist and Shout • When I'm Sixty-Four • and more.
00699562.................................$17.99

Bluegrass
Over 40 classics: Blue Moon of Kentucky • Foggy Mountain Top • High on a Mountain Top • Keep on the Sunny Side • Wabash Cannonball • The Wreck of the Old '97 • and more.
00702585.................................$14.99

Johnny Cash
58 Cash classics: A Boy Named Sue • Cry, Cry, Cry • Daddy Sang Bass • Folsom Prison Blues • I Walk the Line • RIng of Fire • Solitary Man • and more.
00699648................................$17.99

Children's Songs
70 songs for kids: Alphabet Song • Bingo • The Candy Man • Eensy Weensy Spider • Puff the Magic Dragon • Twinkle, Twinkle Little Star • and more.
00699539.................................$16.99

Christmas Carols
80 Christmas carols: Angels We Have Heard on High • The Holly and the Ivy • I Saw Three Ships • Joy to the World • O Holy Night • and more.
00699536.................................$12.99

Christmas Songs
80 songs: All I Want for Christmas Is My Two Front Teeth • Baby, It's Cold Outside • Jingle Bell Rock • Mistletoe and Holly • Sleigh Ride • and more.
00119911................................$14.99

Eric Clapton
75 of Slowhand's finest: I Shot the Sheriff • Knockin' on Heaven's Door • Layla • Strange Brew • Tears in Heaven • Wonderful Tonight • and more.
00699567.................................$19.99

Classic Rock
80 rock essentials: Beast of Burden • Cat Scratch Fever • Hot Blooded • Money • Rhiannon • Sweet Emotion • Walk on the Wild Side • and more.
00699598 ....$18.99

Coffeehouse Hits
57 singer-songwriter hits: Don't Know Why • Hallelujah • Meet Virginia • Steal My Kisses • Torn • Wonderwall • You Learn • and more.
00703318 ....$14.99

Country
80 country standards: Boot Scootin' Boogie • Crazy • Hey, Good Lookin'• Sixteen Tons • Through the Years • Your Cheatin' Heart • and more.
00699534 ....$17.99

Country Favorites
Over 60 songs: Achy Breaky Heart (Don't Tell My Heart) • Brand New Man • Gone Country • The Long Black Veil • Make the World Go Away • and more.
00700609 ....$14.99

Country Hits
40 classics: As Good As I Once Was • Before He Cheats • Cruise • Follow Your Arrow • God Gave Me You • The House That Built Me • Just a Kiss • Making Memories of Us • Need You Now • Your Man • and more.
00140859 ....$14.99

Country Standards
60 songs: By the Time I Get to Phoenix • El Paso • The Gambler • I Fall to Pieces • Jolene • King of the Road • Put Your Hand in the Hand • A Rainy Night in Georgia • and more.
00700608 ....$12.95

Cowboy Songs
Over 60 tunes: Back in the Saddle Again • Happy Trails • Home on the Range • Streets of Laredo • The Yellow Rose of Texas • and more.
00699636 ....$19.99

Creedence Clearwater Revival
34 CCR classics: Bad Moon Rising • Born on the Bayou • Down on the Corner • Fortunate Son • Up Around the Bend • and more.
00701786 ....$16.99

Jim Croce
37 tunes: Bad, Bad Leroy Brown • I Got a Name • I'll Have to Say I Love You in a Song • Operator (That's Not the Way It Feels) • Photographs and Memories • Time in a Bottle • You Don't Mess Around with Jim • and many more.
00148087 ....$14.99

Crosby, Stills & Nash

37 hits: Chicago • Dark Star • Deja Vu • Marrakesh Express • Our House • Southern Cross • Suite: Judy Blue Eyes • Teach Your Children • and more.
00701609.............................$16.99

John Denver

50 favorites: Annie's Song • Leaving on a Jet Plane • Rocky Mountain High • Take Me Home, Country Roads • Thank God I'm a Country Boy • and more.
02501697 ....$17.99

Neil Diamond

50 songs: America • Cherry, Cherry • Cracklin' Rosie • Forever in Blue Jeans • I Am...I Said • Love on the Rocks • Song Sung Blue • Sweet Caroline • and dozens more!
00700606 ....$19.99

Disney

56 super Disney songs: Be Our Guest • Friend like Me • Hakuna Matata • It's a Small World • Under the Sea • A Whole New World • Zip-A-Dee-Doo-Dah • and more.
00701071 ....$17.99

The Doors

60 classics from the Doors: Break on Through to the Other Side • Hello, I Love You (Won't You Tell Me Your Name?) • Light My Fire • Love Her Madly • Riders on the Storm • Touch Me • and more.
00699888 ....$17.99

Eagles

40 familiar songs: Already Gone • Best of My Love • Desperado • Hotel California • Life in the Fast Lane • Peaceful Easy Feeling • Witchy Woman • more.
00122917 ....$16.99

Early Rock

80 classics: All I Have to Do Is Dream • Big Girls Don't Cry • Fever • Itsy Bitsy Teenie Weenie Yellow Polkadot Bikini • Let's Twist Again • Lollipop • and more.
00699916 ....$14.99

Folk Pop Rock

80 songs: American Pie • Dust in the Wind • Me and Bobby McGee • Somebody to Love • Time in a Bottle • and more.
00699651 ....$17.99

Folksongs

80 folk favorites: Aura Lee • Camptown Races • Danny Boy • Man of Constant Sorrow • Nobody Knows the Trouble I've Seen • and more.
00699541 ....$14.99

40 Easy Strumming Songs

Features 40 songs: Cat's in the Cradle • Daughter • Hey, Soul Sister • Homeward Bound • Take It Easy • Wild Horses • and more.
00115972 ....$16.99

Four Chord Songs

40 hit songs: Blowin' in the Wind • I Saw Her Standing There • Should I Stay or Should I Go • Stand by Me • Turn the Page • Wonderful Tonight • and more.
00701611 ....$14.99

Glee

50+ hits: Bad Romance • Beautiful • Dancing with Myself • Don't Stop Believin' • Imagine • Rehab • Teenage Dream • True Colors • and dozens more.
00702501 ....$14.99

Gospel Hymns

80 hymns: Amazing Grace • Give Me That Old Time Religion • I Love to Tell the Story • Shall We Gather at the River? • Wondrous Love • and more.
00700463 ....$14.99

Grand Ole Opry®

80 great songs: Abilene • Act Naturally • Country Boy • Crazy • Friends in Low Places • He Stopped Loving Her Today • Wings of a Dove • dozens more!
00699885 ....$16.95

Grateful Dead

30 favorites: Casey Jones • Friend of the Devil • High Time • Ramble on Rose • Ripple • Rosemary • Sugar Magnolia • Truckin' • Uncle John's Band • more.
00139461 ....$14.99

Green Day

34 faves: American Idiot • Basket Case • Boulevard of Broken Dreams • Good Riddance (Time of Your Life) • 21 Guns • Wake Me Up When September Ends • When I Come Around • and more.
00103074 ....$14.99

Irish Songs

45 Irish favorites: Danny Boy • Girl I Left Behind Me • Harrigan • I'll Tell Me Ma • The Irish Rover • My Wild Irish Rose • When Irish Eyes Are Smiling • and more!
00701044 ....$14.99

Michael Jackson

27 songs: Bad • Beat It • Billie Jean • Black or White (Rap Version) • Don't Stop 'Til You Get Enough • The Girl Is Mine • Man in the Mirror • Rock with You • Smooth Criminal • Thriller • more.
00137847 ....$14.99

Billy Joel

60 Billy Joel favorites: • It's Still Rock and Roll to Me • The Longest Time • Piano Man • She's Always a Woman • Uptown Girl • We Didn't Start the Fire • You May Be Right • and more.
00699632 ....$19.99

Elton John

60 songs: Bennie and the Jets • Candle in the Wind • Crocodile Rock • Goodbye Yellow Brick Road • Sad Songs Say So Much • Tiny Dancer • Your Song • more.
00699732 ....$15.99

Ray LaMontagne

20 songs: Empty • Gossip in the Grain • Hold You in My Arms • I Still Care for You • Jolene • Trouble • You Are the Best Thing • and more.
00130337.............................$12.99

Latin Songs

60 favorites: Bésame Mucho (Kiss Me Much) • The Girl from Ipanema (Garôta De Ipanema) • The Look of Love • So Nice (Summer Samba) • and more.
00700973 ....$14.99

Love Songs

65 romantic ditties: Baby, I'm-A Want You • Fields of Gold • Here, There and Everywhere • Let's Stay Together • Never My Love • The Way We Were • more!
00701043...........................$14.99

Bob Marley

36 songs: Buffalo Soldier • Get up Stand Up • I Shot the Sheriff • Is This Love • No Woman No Cry • One Love • Redemption Song • and more.
00701704.............................$17.99

Bruno Mars

15 hits: Count on Me • Grenade • If I Knew • Just the Way You Are • The Lazy Song • Locked Out of Heaven • Marry You • Treasure • When I Was Your Man • and more.
00125332 ....$12.99

Paul McCartney

60 from Sir Paul: Band on the Run • Jet • Let 'Em In • Maybe I'm Amazed • No More Lonely Nights • Say Say Say • Take It Away • With a Little Luck • and more!
00385035 ....$16.95

Steve Miller

33 hits: Dance Dance Dance • Jet Airliner • The Joker • Jungle Love • Rock'n Me • Serenade from the Stars • Swingtown • Take the Money and Run • and more.
00701146.............................$12.99

Modern Worship

80 modern worship favorites: All Because of Jesus • Amazed • Everlasting God • Happy Day • I Am Free • Jesus Messiah • and more.
00701801 ....$16.99

Motown

60 Motown masterpieces: ABC • Baby I Need Your Lovin' • I'll Be There • Stop! In the Name of Love • You Can't Hurry Love • and more.
00699734 ....$17.99

Willie Nelson

44 favorites: Always on My Mind • Beer for My Horses • Blue Skies • Georgia on My Mind • Help Me Make It Through the Night • On the Road Again • Whiskey River • and many more.
00148273 ....$17.99

Nirvana
40 songs: About a Girl • Come as You Are • Heart Shaped Box • The Man Who Sold the World • Smells like Teen Spirit • You Know You're Right • and more.
00699762 ....$16.99

Roy Orbison
38 songs: Blue Bayou • Oh, Pretty Woman • Only the Lonely (Know the Way I Feel) • Working for the Man • You Got It • and more.
00699752 ....$17.99

Peter, Paul & Mary
43 favorites: If I Had a Hammer (The Hammer Song) • Leaving on a Jet Plane • Puff the Magic Dragon • This Land Is Your Land • and more.
00103013....................................$19.99

Tom Petty
American Girl • Breakdown • Don't Do Me like That • Free Fallin' • Here Comes My Girl • Into the Great Wide Open • Mary Jane's Last Dance • Refugee • Runnin' Down a Dream • The Waiting • and more.
00699883 ....$15.99

Pink Floyd
30 songs: Another Brick in the Wall, Part 2 • Brain Damage • Breathe • Comfortably Numb • Hey You • Money • Mother • Run like Hell • Us and Them • Wish You Were Here • Young Lust • and many more.
00139116 ....$14.99

Pop/Rock
80 chart hits: Against All Odds • Come Sail Away • Every Breath You Take • Hurts So Good • Kokomo • More Than Words • Smooth • Summer of '69 • and more.
00699538 ....$16.99

Praise and Worship
80 favorites: Agnus Dei • He Is Exalted • I Could Sing of Your Love Forever • Lord, I Lift Your Name on High • More Precious Than Silver • Open the Eyes of My Heart • Shine, Jesus, Shine • and more.
00699634 ....$14.99

Elvis Presley
60 hits: All Shook Up • Blue Suede Shoes • Can't Help Falling in Love • Heartbreak Hotel • Hound Dog • Jailhouse Rock • Suspicious Minds • Viva Las Vegas • and more.
00699633 ....$17.99

Queen
40 hits: Bohemian Rhapsody • Crazy Little Thing Called Love • Fat Bottomed Girls • Killer Queen • Tie Your Mother Down • Under Pressure • You're My Best Friend • and more!
00702395 ....$14.99

Red Hot Chili Peppers
50 hits: Californication • Give It Away • Higher Ground • Love Rollercoaster • Scar Tissue • Suck My Kiss • Under the Bridge • and more.
00699710 ....$19.99

The Rolling Stones
35 hits: Angie • Beast of Burden • Fool to Cry • Happy • It's Only Rock 'N' Roll (But I Like It) • Miss You • Not Fade Away • Respectable • Rocks Off • Start Me Up • Time Is on My Side • Tumbling Dice • Waiting on a Friend • and more.
00137716 ....$17.99

Bob Seger
41 favorites: Against the Wind • Hollywood Nights • Katmandu • Like a Rock • Night Moves • Old Time Rock & Roll • You'll Accomp'ny Me • and more!
00701147....................................$12.99

Carly Simon
Nearly 40 classic hits, including: Anticipation • Haven't Got Time for the Pain • Jesse • Let the River Run • Nobody Does It Better • You're So Vain • and more.
00121011....................................$14.99

Sting
50 favorites from Sting and the Police: Don't Stand So Close to Me • Every Breath You Take • Fields of Gold • King of Pain • Message in a Bottle • Roxanne • and more.
00699921 ....$17.99

Taylor Swift
40 tunes: Back to December • Bad Blood • Blank Space • Fearless • Fifteen • I Knew You Were Trouble • Look What You Made Me Do • Love Story • Mean • Shake It Off • Speak Now • Wildest Dreams • and many more.
00263755....................................$16.99

Three Chord Acoustic Songs
30 acoustic songs: All Apologies • Blowin' in the Wind • Hold My Hand • Just the Way You Are • Ring of Fire • Shelter from the Storm • This Land Is Your Land • and more.
00123860 ....$14.99

Three Chord Songs
65 includes: All Right Now • La Bamba • Lay Down Sally • Mony, Mony • Rock Around the Clock • Rock This Town • Werewolves of London • You Are My Sunshine • and more.
00699720 ....$17.99

Two-Chord Songs
Nearly 60 songs: ABC • Brick House • Eleanor Rigby • Fever • Paperback Writer • Ramblin' Man Tulsa Time • When Love Comes to Town • and more.
00119236....................................$16.99

U2
40 U2 songs: Beautiful Day • Mysterious Ways • New Year's Day • One • Sunday Bloody Sunday • Walk On • Where the Streets Have No Name • With or Without You • and more.
00137744....................................$14.99

Hank Williams
68 classics: Cold, Cold Heart • Hey, Good Lookin' • Honky Tonk Blues • I'm a Long Gone Daddy • Jambalaya (On the Bayou) • Your Cheatin' Heart • and more.
00700607 ....$16.99

Stevie Wonder
40 of Stevie's best: For Once in My Life • Higher Ground • Isn't She Lovely • My Cherie Amour • Sir Duke • Superstition • Uptight (Everything's Alright) • Yester-Me, Yester-You, Yesterday • and more!
00120862 ....$14.99

HAL•LEONARD®

Prices, contents and availability subject to change without notice.

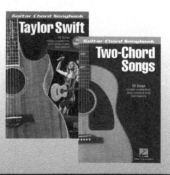